647.95 Chm
Chmelynski, Carol Ann Caprione,
1950-
Opportunities in food service
careers /

34028058125155
SHO$13.95 ocm58788970

3 4028 05812 5155
HARRIS COUNTY PUBLIC LIBRARY

in

Food Service Careers

Discards

D0840982

OPPORTUNITIES

in

Food Service Careers

REVISED EDITION

CAROL CAPRIONE CHMELYNSKI

McGraw·Hill

New York   Chicago   San Francisco   Lisbon   London   Madrid   Mexico City
Milan   New Delhi   San Juan   Seoul   Singapore   Sydney   Toronto

The **McGraw·Hill** Companies

Library of Congress Cataloging-in-Publication Data

Chmelynski, Carol Ann Caprione, 1950–
    Opportunities in food service careers / Carol Caprione Chmelynski. — Rev. ed.
        p.   cm.
    ISBN 0-07-144850-0
    1. Food service—Vocational guidance.   I. Title.

    TX911.3.V62 C45   2005
    647.95′023—dc22   2005008879

Copyright © 2006 by The McGraw-Hill Companies, Inc. All rights reserved. Printed in the United States of America. Except as permitted under the United States Copyright Act of 1976, no part of this publication may be reproduced or distributed in any form or by any means, or stored in a database or retrieval system, without the prior written permission of the publisher.

1 2 3 4 5 6 7 8 9 0   DOC/DOC   0 9 8 7 6 5

ISBN 0-07-144850-0

Interior design by Rattray Design

McGraw-Hill books are available at special quantity discounts to use as premiums and sales promotions, or for use in corporate training programs. For more information, please write to the Director of Special Sales, Professional Publishing, McGraw-Hill, Two Penn Plaza, New York, NY 10121-2298. Or contact your local bookstore.

This book is printed on acid-free paper.

Contents

The largest retail employer. The four main branches.

A variety of jobs and careers. Industry growth potential. Career ladders. Opportunities for women and minorities. Salaries. Additional benefits. Food service career flexibility. Personality traits. Work attitudes. Ability to handle stress.

Foreword

By ANY MEASURE, the food service industry has enjoyed tremendous success over the past three decades, and projections for the future point to even greater growth in the twenty-first century. The reasons for this favorable forecast include the following:

- A shift from a manufacturing-based economy to a service-based economy
- More working women and more workers per household, which causes more people to eat away from home and pick up (or have delivered) food prepared away from home
- A more active, mobile population
- Increasing personal disposable income of Americans, particularly those age fifty-five and over

If you stop to think about all the places outside the home where food is prepared and/or served, you can begin to sense the size and the growth of the food service industry and, by extension, the growth of careers in food service. Not only do people eat meals in tablecloth restaurants, but they can also eat in fast-food establishments, in coffee shops and cafeterias, in high schools and colleges, in convention halls and sports stadiums, in recreation and amusement parks, on planes, in trains, in hospitals and nursing homes, in shopping malls and department stores, everywhere that people congregate. While many people eat about twenty-one meals a week (seven days, three meals a day), nearly one-third to one-half or more of these meals are taken outside the home. And that trend is surging upward.

What an employment and career opportunity! What an opportunity for growth in a growing industry! There has never been a better time for energetic, caring people to start on a food service career, and there are so many occupations from which to choose. You can work in the "heart of the house" such as the kitchen area, in the "front of the house" such as the service area, or in the "pulse of the house" such as the office. You can work for a large company or a small restaurant or anything in between. The diversity is tremendous. There are no limits on your potential for growth and success in the food service industry. The opportunities abound. Go for them!

William P. Fisher, Ph.D.
Executive Vice President
National Restaurant Association

PREFACE

THROUGHOUT THIS BOOK you will find much useful information on a variety of careers in the food service industry. Because no book covering such a broad field could provide all the information you need, you should look to the appendixes for additional resources. Appendix A features contact information, including website addresses, for a range of professional associations. Professional associations are key sources for all the latest news in the field. In addition, they often offer job postings and career prospects, scholarships and grants, and educational and training opportunities. Appendix B contains a list of industry journals and magazines with links to either their publisher's website or the online version of the magazine itself, where possible.

Surfing the Internet is a wonderful way to discover valuable information that will help you make an informed career choice. This book has been revised to include plenty of online information and links to help you do just that. May your searches be fruitful!

Acknowledgments

The author wishes to acknowledge the invaluable assistance of The Educational Foundation of the National Restaurant Association in Chicago, Illinois, and the National Restaurant Association in Washington, DC, in the preparation of previous editions of this book.

1

THE FOOD SERVICE INDUSTRY

IT IS AN understatement to say that the food service industry is a vast sector that employs many people. In fact, the restaurant industry alone employs approximately eleven million people, making it the largest U.S. employer outside the federal government! And that is just one segment of the food service industry. This field offers qualified, enthusiastic, hardworking people many unique and diverse opportunities for personal growth and areas to work in.

Before we dive into a discussion of the various employment options open to you in this field, it is important to first understand what food service means. The term *food service* applies to establishments that prepare food for others' consumption, typically outside the home. These food service establishments include:

- Restaurants of every kind, such as cafeterias, carryout operations, coffee shops, fast-food chains, sandwich shops, and white-tablecloth operations

- Food preparation facilities in clubs, spas, cocktail lounges, hotels, convention centers and sports arenas, supermarkets, and taverns
- Airline, railroad, and cruise ship operations
- Institutional food service, including school and college, hospital, industrial, military, and retirement-home food service
- The subset of specialty stores and supermarkets that sell gourmet and diet food to go

The Largest Retail Employer

Food service workers are one of the largest and fastest-growing occupational groups in the nation's labor force. In fact, more than three times as many people work in food service than in automobile manufacturing and steel manufacturing combined. The food service industry prepares one-fifth of all food produced in the United States. That's forty billion pounds of food served during the course of nearly two hundred million customer transactions each day.

According to the U.S. Department of Labor, Bureau of Labor Statistics, 4 percent of all employed men, 6 percent of all employed women, and 20 percent of all employed teenagers work in food-preparation and food service occupations. By the year 2006, the food service industry will need 2.3 million more people than it now employs. Food service opportunities will continue to expand because the number of working couples and singles continues to grow; this demographic factor means there will be an increased demand for food prepared away from home. After reading this book, you will discover that job opportunities exist almost everywhere and for almost any interested person, including those who have limited skills or little formal education.

The food service industry is a growing one. In 1973 there were 490,000 establishments. In 1977 that number increased to 535,000. In 1982 it was 559,000, in 1991 it was 657,000, and in 1998 it was 797,000. And that number continues to grow. Consumers are spending a growing proportion of their food dollars away from home. Food service industry sales increased dramatically in the 1970s, rising from $42.8 billion in 1970 to $119.6 billion in 1980. In 1988 industry sales were $211.8 billion. In 1991 food service sales were $248.1 billion. Today's sales in this area top an astounding $275 billion annually.

The Four Main Branches

Food service is an industry made up of vast numbers of establishments that are as diverse in atmosphere as the food prepared and sold in them. No matter what your area of culinary interest, you are sure to find a job preparing (or selling or marketing) food in an environment that interests you. Not only is the type of food prepared unique to each establishment, but there is also great diversity in the clientele served. There are many ways to define the components of the food service industry, but it is perhaps easiest to categorize the industry into four main branches: commercial, institutional, military, and charitable feeding.

Commercial Feeding

The commercial feeding group comprises those establishments that are open to the public, are operated for profit, and that may operate facilities and/or supply meal service on a regular basis for others. Commercial feeding accounts for nearly 74 percent of industry sales and includes restaurants, food service contractors, hotel restaurants, coffee shops, and restaurants in department stores, airports, and so forth. Keep in mind, however, the types of commercial feeding establishments described here are to some extent arbitrary, and restaurant categories rarely have neat, sharp boundaries.

There are many different types of commercial feeding establishments that fall into several categories.

Fast-Food Restaurants

These types of restaurant primarily sell limited refreshments and prepared food items such as fish, hamburger, chicken, or roast beef sandwiches for consumption either on or near the premises or for take-home. In recent years, in response to the current epidemic of obesity in the United States, fast-food restaurants have added salads and leaner options to their menus. The fast-food restaurant is inexpensive, appeals to all ages, and is suitable for snack service as well as meal service. Seating is available, but customers may order and pick up the food at the counter. Fast-food restaurants are primarily chain or franchise units, and they are very familiar to the general public. Some examples include Subway (www.subway.com), McDonald's (www.mcdonalds.com), Burger King (www.bk.com), Papa John's (www.papajohns.com), and White Castle (www.white castle.com), among others.

People who work in fast-food restaurants perform a variety of jobs, including preparing the food, which can usually be quickly heated or fried and assembled following a standard format; tidying the premises; taking orders; and handling money. There are generally several of these workers at a fast-food restaurant and one or two managers. Managers either have had previous managerial experience or they have worked their way up to the position by showing initiative and drive. Workers at fast-food establishments need no formal training, making this a good job for high school students or those without additional education or training.

Cafeterias

These feeding establishments serve prepared food and beverages usually through a cafeteria line, where customers make selections from a display of items. There may be some limited waiter or waitress service. Table and/or booth seating facilities are usually provided. Cost is typically low to moderate. Cafeterias that are open to the public can be found in such places as hospitals, college campuses, and office and government buildings.

Most people working in cafeterias are behind the scenes in the kitchen doing prep work, cooking, and dishwashing. Cashiers and workers who clear the tables interact with patrons in the dining area. These jobs require no education or experience, making them easy to obtain for people lacking in either of these areas.

Family-Type Restaurants

These are the types of restaurants you might frequent with your family, spouse, or friends for a casual meal. The atmosphere is likely to be relaxed and unpretentious, and service is fast. In most cases, reservations are not necessary. This kind of operation is well-known and the most used, especially during meal hours, and it generally features no-frills comfort food. Denny's (www.dennys.com) or Big Boy (www.bigboy.com) restaurants are chains that are good examples of this type of establishment.

In the family restaurant, you will find servers, hosts or hostesses, managers, buspersons, dishwashers, cooks, line cooks, and prep cooks. These workers often make up the backbone of the food service industry, and they can be found in a variety of restaurants, including atmosphere and gourmet restaurants. Typically, these workers, with the exception of the manager and perhaps some of the cooks, do not need previous experience to work in a family restaurant, making this kind of establishment an excellent place to gain experience. This is also a good place to work if you are in high school or college, have no previous experience, or if you want a more low-key environment to work in.

Atmosphere Restaurants

These restaurants create an atmosphere by virtue of setting, decor, historic context, special artifacts, or view. Although you might take your family, you would probably have a special reason for patronizing this type of restaurant. Family-friendly restaurants, such as the Hard Rock Café (www.hardrock.com) chain or Chuck E. Cheese's (www.chuckecheese.com) are also included in this group.

The atmosphere restaurant typically employs the same types of workers as does the family restaurant, but it may also have a special section attached to the restaurant that sells souvenirs, including hats, T-shirts, mugs, and the like. Salespeople who work the gift shop do not need any experience in food service, but they may need previous sales experience. In addition, some atmosphere restaurants feature live entertainment as part of their attraction. Waitstaff will have to learn to work in what may be a bustling and lively environment that may also be quite loud. On the other hand, if the restaurant's main attraction is of a more historic nature, it is likely to be more sedate and formal.

Gourmet Restaurants

One would patronize gourmet restaurants because the food, service, and gracious atmosphere contribute to a refined dining experience. It is more formal than the family or atmosphere restaurant, and it is characterized by an unhurried pace. This type of restaurant might be selected for a special occasion or perhaps because good food and service on a particular dining-out occasion are sought. Charlie Trotter's (www.charlietrotters.com) in Chicago and Nobu (www.noburestaurants.com) in New York, Miami, Malibu, Las Vegas, and around the world are fine gourmet restaurants.

Gourmet restaurants are wonderful places to work because the atmosphere is typically tranquil, the pace is slower with tables turning every two hours or so, and the compensation is excellent. Because there are so many perks to working in this type of restaurant, there are also many requirements. The same types of workers are employed in the gourmet restaurant as the family-style restaurant, yet these workers often have many years of experience working in increasingly more prestigious restaurants.

The waitstaff is expected to have a thorough knowledge of wine, including pairing it with food in order to make recommendations, and be able to describe unique kinds of food and styles of preparation. Oftentimes, the owner may also be the head chef. Those assisting him or her in the kitchen will need formal training from a culinary school as well as experience. The maître d' in a gourmet restaurant is in charge of the "front of the house," or the dining area. This person's job is to make sure that people are seated quickly, the staff is properly attentive to the patrons, and the atmosphere and the overall dining experience is perfect. He or she also handles any problems that arise. The sommelier is a wine expert in charge of stocking and ordering wines for the restaurant, creating a wine list, and helping patrons pair wine with food. In the past, one person held the maître d' and sommelier positions concurrently. Today, however, they are typically two different jobs. Some restaurants may also have a maître fromager—an expert in cheese. For these last few positions, special training is required.

Spas and Resorts

These are upscale, all-in-one vacation or fitness destinations that cater to a more affluent clientele. They feature a variety of recreation and leisure activities, including pools, golf courses, fitness activities, salon services, and massage, to name just a few of the more common amenities. In addition, lodging tends to be refined; there are almost always amazing grounds and some rooms have spectacular views. Restaurants on the premises usually provide all meals, including dine-in and room-service options. The food tends to be fine cuisine, and spas generally focus on healthier options.

Workers in spas and resorts are similar to those in a fine dining establishment. One difference is that some spas or resorts are located in destination areas that may be more popular during certain times of the year. Others are found in places where the climate is temperate year-round. Some spas and resorts offer onsite or nearby lodging for their workers. These are beautiful places to work, and for those who have a touch of the wanderlust, they are good places to earn money.

Cruise Ships

Today, the cruise ship industry is one of the fastest-growing job sectors in the world. Ten to twenty new luxury liners are being built every year. With that growth, there has been an equally impressive boom in the number of available jobs. Operating as giant hotels on water with casinos and theaters thrown into the mix, these ocean-going megaliners employ hundreds of people to work a variety of positions. The top five largest North American cruise lines are

Royal Caribbean (www.royalcaribbean.com/gohome.do), Carnival (www.carnival.com), Princess (www.princess.com), Cunard (www.cunard.com), and Costa (www.costacruise.com). In addition to applying directly to the cruise line, do not overlook concessionaire and placement companies, which are responsible for hiring a large percentage of cruise ship employees, including food and beverage staff.

Positions in food service on cruise ships are similar to those of the other areas we have already discussed. The major difference between land-based establishments and working on a cruise ship is that the work tends to be seasonal, depending on the route of the ship. For example, cruise ships traveling to Alaska will be busy only between May and August, whereas those traveling to China, India, and Southeast Asia will be busiest from November to March. Of course, there are areas, such as Mexico, the Caribbean, and the Amazon, that are busy year-round. Whether you're a college student looking for a unique experience between school years, or anyone else seeking a break from the ordinary office environment, you'll find plenty of opportunities with cruise companies, large or small.

Other

In addition to the establishments already discussed, there are the numerous miscellaneous commercial food service operations that don't fall conveniently into any of these categories. These include coffee shops; diners; food stands; vendors, such as those found in sporting arenas and selling ice cream in the park; and the take-out restaurant, which is typically a small rib, pizza, burger, or hot dog joint. In essence, anywhere you go, you're likely to have the option of buying food, and any place food is offered is a potential site of employment.

Institutional Feeding

The institutional feeding group is composed of business, educational, government, and institutional organizations that operate food services specifically for their workers or those who use their services. Areas of employment range from nursing homes and hospitals to elementary schools and correctional facilities. In institutions, food is provided as an auxiliary service necessary to support the organization's other activities. Although some establishments operate for profit, this is not the aim of the institutional food service activity. Rather, such institutions serve food principally as a convenience for their own employees, students, patients, and the like.

Institutional settings employ the same food preparation, retail, and cleanup workers as do other food service establishments. Little education or experience is required for most of these positions, with the exception of perhaps the cook or kitchen manager. Some places, such as schools and hospitals, may employ dietitians, whose job is to design healthful meals for those being served. Employment as a dietitian requires a college education.

Military Feeding

The Continental Congress established the first formal military food program in 1775. Today, military feeding comprises the sale of food and beverages at officers' and enlisted persons' clubs and military exchanges, as well as food service to troops in a defense capacity. The military serves food to hundreds of thousands of service members every day in any one of the five military branches: the U.S. Army, Navy, Air Force, Marine Corps, and Coast Guard. In fact, more than one million meals are prepared in military kitchens every day. Some of these kitchens prepare thousands of meals at one time, while others prepare food for small groups of people. Regardless of the scale, meals must be carefully planned and prepared to ensure good nutrition and variety.

Numerous individuals in a variety of positions have a hand in feeding U.S. troops and their families. Food service specialists—sometimes called mess management specialists—prepare all types of food according to standard and dietetic recipes. They also order and inspect food supplies and prepare meats for cooking. In addition, approximately five hundred food service managers direct the facilities that prepare and serve food. All of these individuals are also members of the military branch for which they work, with all of the benefits and obligations that entails.

There are a variety of websites you can visit for additional information, including the Army Center of Excellence (www.quarter master.army.mil/aces/index.html), Army Food Service Program (www.qmfound.com/food.htm), Research and Development Associates for Military Food and Packaging Systems (www.military food.org), Today's Military (www.todaysmilitary.com), and the United States Department of Defense (www.defenselink.mil). Another fascinating website worth mentioning is dedicated to the services and meals that military chefs and bakers provide for their fellow military members. The Subsistence and Army Cooks History Page at www.qmfound.com/army_subsistence_history.htm offers detailed information about the army's food service program today and throughout U.S. history, including the Civil War. Not only will you learn about the history of military food service, but you may also learn some tricks of the trade and recipes from this informative site.

Charitable Feeding

According to the World Health Organization (www.who.int/en), hunger and malnutrition claim an astounding ten million lives around the world every year, which breaks down to twenty-five thousand lives every day or one life every five seconds. Given this staggering amount of need, there are innumerable ways for you to help organizations—large and small, global and national—feed the hungry. Perhaps the most rewarding jobs working in charitable feeding operations are the volunteer positions delivering or serving food to the hungry or homebound. There are also paying positions, which are found mostly in the corporate headquarters. These positions generally have nothing to do with food preparation. Instead, they are usually jobs shipping food or working at a desk getting the word out about the charity and fund-raising. On occasion, however, nutritionists are employed to help ensure that the selection and combination of foods chosen are nutritious and well balanced. In an organization like the Chicago Food Depository (www.chicagos foodbank.org), for example, a nutritionist may have even greater responsibilities, including providing nutrition training and education to agencies that feed the hungry, assisting in developing a nutrition curriculum, and teaching classes on topics related to nutrition to agency staff and volunteers.

Many local food banks are run by a parent organization. For example, America's Second Harvest (www.secondharvest.org) is a domestic hunger relief organization that runs a network of nearly two hundred food banks, distributing food to twenty-six million hungry Americans each year. Food banks and pantries and national organizations like Meals on Wheels (www.mowaa.org) are probably your best bets for employment, since there are more of them to be found across the country. Other major organizations include Freedom from Hunger (www.freefromhunger.org), Global Impact (www.charity.org), Mercy Corps (www.mercycorps.org/home), Oxfam America (www.oxfamamerica.org), Unicef (www.unicef

usa.org), United Nations World Food Programme (www.wfp.org), and World Hunger Year (www.worldhungeryear.org). Searching online, through the Yellow Pages, and asking your local librarian to help you locate organizations should yield a wealth of employment possibilities.

You're probably getting excited about the vast number and kinds of job options available to you in the food service industry. Now that you know a little bit about the breadth of the industry, the next step is to find out about its career outlook, including potential for growth and compensation and benefits, and whether you have the personality to make it in this industry. Later chapters will provide you with details about the range of positions found in the food service industry. Read on!

2

Food Service Industry Career Outlook

A POSITION IN the food service industry offers many exciting prospects for growth and personal satisfaction. Working in food service helps you to meet one of society's basic needs—the need for food. And working for either a charitable organization or the government in planning and preparing foods for schoolchildren and members of the military may give you a great sense of satisfaction in that what you're doing is tangibly benefiting someone.

In the United States today, our relationship to food is more complex than being merely one of meeting basic needs. People use food in a variety of ways, including as a form of entertainment, as a way to celebrate special events and occasions, and in our courtship rituals (think of the old adage "the way to a man's heart is through his stomach!"). In this case, the work you do will bring joy to people, which can also give you great satisfaction.

A Variety of Jobs and Careers

Almost any interested person, including people who have limited skills or little formal education, can find a niche in the food service industry. This is an industry that offers good job prospects and potential to people with all levels of formal education and on-the-job training. For the high school graduate, a career in food service is an immediate possibility. Further academic training in community colleges or in four-year college or university programs greatly expands career potential in jobs with greater responsibility and higher pay. In addition, the food service industry provides opportunities for people of virtually all ages. For sixteen-year-old high school students as well as adults beginning or changing a career, finding employment in the food service industry can be an excellent choice. Basically, there's a job for everyone in food service.

There are no formal educational requirements for many food service jobs, and skills are often learned through on-the-job training. Many restaurants hire inexperienced people as dining room attendants, sanitation/maintenance workers, counter workers, waiters, waitresses, and bartenders. However, experience sometimes is necessary to obtain one of these positions in a large or upscale restaurant or catering firm. Previous employment in a food service occupation, such as kitchen helper or assistant cook, often is necessary to secure a job as a cook. Experienced workers may advance to food service manager, maître d'hôtel, headwaiter, or chef. Upper-level positions usually require academic training and on-the-job experience. While the amount of career preparation you have determines your entry level into the food service field, the depth and breadth of the field guarantees you ample room for upward movement. (Education and training will be explored in greater detail in Chapter 8.)

Industry Growth Potential

Food service is a growing and thriving industry. According to the Bureau of Labor Statistics, employment growth in the food service industry will outpace that for most other industries through 2006. In fact, employment in service-producing industries will increase faster than average, with growth near 30 percent! This strong job growth potential is the result of the following factors:

- Expansion in the industry, particularly the fast-food segment
- The aging of the U.S. population
- Higher average incomes
- More leisure time
- An increase in one- and two-person households
- A continued increase in the number of working women

All of these demographic trends are expected to increase the number of people who go out to eat, thus creating a demand for more workers to serve restaurant patrons in the coming years. In addition to growth in demand for workers, thousands of job openings will occur each year because of the relatively high turnover rate in the industry, which will largely be the result of students working part-time. That means that there are likely to be good job opportunities in your area.

The food service industry is the primary retail employer in the United States. More than ten million people have found their careers in food service. Each year, more than three hundred thousand new employees will be needed to supply the growing demand for the industry's services. Through good economic times and bad, this growth has remained steady, making a career in food service a career with a stable future.

Career Ladders

The food service industry is now, more than ever, interested in training and retraining personnel who are qualified for food service careers, motivated to perform, and interested in staying on the job. More and more food service operations have implemented a career development system to assure their personnel that there are no dead-end jobs in their area. On-the-job training that provides restaurant employees with a systematic and visible way of moving up in the field is a key concern of many restaurant owners and operators. As in other professions, the sequence of jobs through which food service employees can be promoted is commonly referred to as a career ladder.

Career ladders link together jobs that use similar skills and knowledge, thus providing opportunities for upward movement of employees within one field. While you will gain new skills and knowledge with each new job up the career ladder, you should view every position as preparation for a more challenging and higher prestige position. An example of someone progressing up a career ladder is a person hired as a short-order cook, who is then promoted to kitchen helper, cook, executive cook, and finally, chef. Of course, sometimes it may be necessary to change the place of employment to achieve higher positions. Keep in mind that many of the food service skills are interrelated, and you should never let the opportunity to learn new skills pass you by.

You will achieve greater job satisfaction and peace of mind if you have a clear idea of both your short- and long-term goals. Try mapping out on a piece of paper your future job goals and plans. Start by writing down the ideal job for you. Then write down the answers to the following questions:

- What jobs must you work before you can get to your ideal job?
- What kind of education or training is required for each position?
- How long will it take you to complete the education or training?
- How will you pay for it and what positions can you work in the meantime?
- How long should you work at each position before you've achieved sufficient mastery to allow you to move forward?

Completing this exercise provides you with the framework for thinking about and creating your short- and long-term career goals. By identifying exactly what jobs you want to attain and what it takes to achieve them, you will be better prepared to accomplish your career goals in a timely fashion.

Opportunities for Women and Minorities

Historically, women and minority owners and managers of food service businesses have been underrepresented in the industry and have encountered many barriers to entrepreneurship. Banks and credit lenders were less willing to provide funding to these demographics than to white males. Because of this, the advantages of franchising were particularly attractive to minorities and women. As a franchisee, a new small business owner obtains a network of suppliers and an established brand that carries product reputation and loyalty; these strengths make it more comfortable for lending institutions to provide needed funding.

Still, minority- and women-owned franchises continue to lag far behind their male, white-owned counterparts. While minorities today comprise more than one-fourth of the American population, a recent U.S. Small Business Administration study showed that minorities own less than 10 percent of franchises.

To address this concern, several of the largest franchisor companies began to develop formal programs to help increase the number of minority-owned establishments. In 1982, Kentucky Fried Chicken (www.kfc.com) created a Minority Franchise Program in which the company provides guarantees for bank loans, thus reducing the needed start-up capital requirements. Other large franchisors in the food service industry, including McDonald's (www.mcdonalds.com), Burger King (www.bk.com), Wendy's (www.wendys.com), Ben and Jerry's (www.benjerry.com), and Denny's (www.dennys.com), initiated similar programs. Most of these programs include mechanisms to ease access to start-up capital and to provide franchise operational training, and many also provide franchise site assistance, minority peer support groups, and other forms of assistance. While these programs initially targeted African-American entrepreneurs, they later added other minorities and women to their focus. (Franchises will be discussed in greater detail in Chapter 7.)

In general, women and minorities today are well represented in all job categories throughout the food service industry. Indeed, their share of jobs continues to steadily rise. The U.S. Department of Labor, Bureau of Labor Statistics reports employment of African-Americans and Latinos in food service is climbing at approximately twice the rate for all industries combined. Today, the food service industry employs more women and minorities as managers than any other industry. Many restaurant chains even offer special training programs for new women and minority employees and provide role models to guide them in their careers.

Salaries

Wages and salaries for some of the most popular food service occupations are given in Table 2.1. The figures shown come from the U.S. Department of Labor, Bureau of Labor Statistics, in a 2002 report.

Information on the earning potential of careers not mentioned here will be found in later chapters.

Table 2.1 Wages and Salaries for Food Service Occupations, U.S. Department of Labor Statistics, 2002

Occupation	Hourly Wage	Annual Mean Salary
Bartenders	$7.21*	
Waiters/waitresses	$6.80*	
Buspersons	$6.26**	
Hosts/Hostesses	$7.36**	
Chefs	$13.43	
Cooks, restaurant	$9.16	
institution or cafeteria	$8.72	
short-order	$7.82	
fast-food	$6.90	
Meat cutters	$11.40	
Managers		$35,790 (not paid hourly)
Dietitians		$41,170 (not paid hourly)

*Tips usually average between 10 and 20 percent of patrons' bills.
**These employees may receive a percentage of waiters' and waitresses' tips.

Additional Benefits

Salary is not the only area where the food service industry is competitive with other industries. Skyrocketing health care costs make out-of-pocket insurance premiums nearly unaffordable to the average family, so having a benefits package that includes insurance through your company is a big perk. In addition, less tangible benefits include things like flexible hours, vacation and sick time, and discounts on food. Benefits will vary from organization to organization, but some fringe benefits may include the following:

- Meals for free while working
- Free uniforms
- Paid vacation
- Paid holidays
- Paid sick leave
- Medical insurance
- Dental insurance
- Group life insurance
- Accidental death and dismemberment insurance
- Profit sharing/401K savings plan
- Pension plan
- Stock purchase discounts or free stock
- Education assistance or tuition reimbursement

Depending on your situation, some benefits may be more appealing to you than others. Working parents or those going to school and working will have different needs. Regardless, you should carefully consider what each position has to offer apart from wages and salary.

Food Service Career Flexibility

If your life schedule changes from day to day or is often hard to nail down, then a job in certain areas of food service will be great for you. Of course, many jobs have set hours each week, especially those in the military and those for dietitians, but others are more flexible. In addition, food service occupations are found in abundance in every part of the country, urban and rural, so you are sure to find some form of employment to suit your needs.

Location

The food service industry offers employment in every city and town in the country. Keep in mind that while the pay scale for many jobs is higher in the larger metropolitan cities than in smaller towns, so is the cost of living. A benefit of living and working in an urban setting is that there tend to be more opportunities for higher prestige jobs such as chefs, sommeliers, maître d's, and dietitians. You are likely to gain more experience and move more quickly up the career ladder in these settings.

Hours

Because restaurants are open from early in the morning to late at night, and some are even open all night, a job in food service can meet anyone's schedule needs. The flexibility of the hours is especially appealing to students, young parents, and anyone who desires part-time work. Your hours can either be set or vary from week to week. Oftentimes, weekends will be mandatory, although if you give enough notice, you can typically get someone to cover a shift for you in the event that you have other plans. Picking up extra shifts to make more money is also an option for many jobs in food service.

Work Styles

In food service, there is both a place for people to lead others with their creativity, supervisory, and management skills as well as a place for those who prefer to follow such leaders. A career in food service can mean a job with little responsibility or a job with a great deal of responsibility; either way, the job will be a secure one. It really depends on what you are willing to take on. Do you want to be a leader, or would you rather relinquish the task to others? In any event, working in this industry requires teamwork. The food service industry truly does offer something for everyone's needs.

Personality Traits

Part of making a good career decision is knowing yourself well and understanding the job you're considering. Assessing your talents and skills is crucial to determining whether you will make a good fit with a particular job and whether you will derive satisfaction from it. To do this, you must first know what kinds of skills and personality traits are best suited to a career in food service. Then you can determine whether you possess some of these traits. You need not possess all of them to make a good fit in this field, but if you don't possess any, you may want to rethink your decision to enter the food service industry.

Food service is a people business. Thus a pleasing personality is vital to success in this field. Interacting and working with many different types of people is the nature of the industry, so to succeed, a food service worker must possess the following qualities:

- Friendliness
- Diplomacy
- Helpfulness
- Attentiveness
- Humor
- Sympathy
- Enthusiasm
- Creativity

As stated before, opportunities to gain experience and training are excellent; however, the ambition to use these opportunities as a means to advance up the career ladder is a vital attribute to achieving true success in this field.

Work Attitudes

People who do well in food service careers possess some of the qualities previously described and more that contribute to their advancement in the field. In addition to the above, you must be a hard worker who is willing to put time and effort into doing work that often goes unrecognized. You must be interested in food, the preparing and enjoyment of it, as well as the nutritional value of it. You must not be averse to working with people because you will constantly interact with people in this industry. This does not mean that you have to be an extrovert, just that you cannot be a misanthrope. Finally, there is no substitute for a positive work attitude, which includes the following basics:

- Punctuality
- Pride in personal appearance
- Businesslike manner

- Eagerness to learn
- Willingness to work
- Ability to accept criticism and direction

Ability to Handle Stress

Because every food service operation involves peak periods and deadlines leading up to them, pressures can be intense. A healthy mental outlook that enables individuals to function well with fellow workers while serving the public effectively is a must. Good physical condition is also often necessary, because much of your time may be spent on your feet and lifting heavy items.

The major goal of every food service operation is the satisfaction of the food service customer. The people who choose to work in the industry must recognize this goal and dedicate themselves to its achievement. It can be very stressful when a customer is upset and reacting emotionally or aggressively, but you must maintain the calm and cool necessary to diffuse the situation, so that the customer walks away with only positive things to say about your organization. The phrase "the customer is always right" is the motto of the food service industry.

A career in food service is a demanding one, but it can provide many rewards. If you enjoy meeting, working with, and serving people, then you are well suited to working in this business.

The following chapters cover a range of positions in the food service industry. Brief descriptions of the type of work that each position entails, where you might expect to work, level of compensation, and education and training required will be given. Because you have to start somewhere, the next chapter presents entry-level jobs in the food service industry.

3

Entry-Level Positions

Entry-level positions make up the backbone of the food service industry. Entry-level restaurant workers are the front line of customer service in restaurants, coffee shops, and other food service establishments. They greet customers, escort them to seats, hand out menus, and serve food and beverages. They also answer questions and keep tables and dining areas clean and set for new diners. Busing tables, making salads, and taking care of the soda machine are positions of responsibility that help keep the establishment running smoothly.

Those working in food processing occupations fill the behind-the-scenes entry-level positions. These workers cut, process, bake, and ship a variety of foodstuffs—from meat to sweets—to restaurants, grocery stores, and other retail outlets. Almost all food service workers, no matter what their environment, work as part of a team, helping coworkers during busy times to improve workflow and customer service.

Food service positions in the military are yet another option. This is a good choice for those who want a stable income and job security. The military offers additional perks like tuition assistance in return for service and training and education in the culinary arts and sciences. However, this is a job that requires significantly more long-term commitment than do the other jobs described in this chapter. Seek out additional information from the sources listed in the appendixes of this book, and talk to a recruiter to make an informed decision.

In this chapter, you will learn about a variety of entry-level positions. In general, these positions require a minimum of training and little to no education. These jobs may be stepping-stones to your long-term career goal, or you may find that one of these is a job you will hold for many years. Regardless of your goals, this chapter will give you the information you need to make a good choice.

Training and Education

There are generally no specific educational or training requirements for entry-level jobs. While many employers prefer to hire high school graduates for host and hostess positions, a high school diploma is usually not required for fast-food workers, counter attendants, dishwashers, dining room attendants, bartender assistants, food preparation workers, and food processing workers. Many employers will also hire applicants who speak little or no English for some of these positions, especially if they have limited verbal contact with the public.

For all of these jobs, workers must be in good physical condition and have physical stamina because they stand most of the time, lift and carry trays, and work at a fast pace during busy periods. Because some jobs come into close physical contact with the public, workers in these positions should be neat in appearance, maintain good personal hygiene, and generally have a pleasant disposition.

An entry-level job in the restaurant division of the food service industry often serves as a source of immediate income—rather than a career—for many people. Many entrants to these jobs are in their late teens or early twenties and have a high school education or less. Usually, they have little or no work experience and many are full-time students or homemakers. These jobs are a major source of part-time employment for high school and college students. In fact, most restaurant jobs are part-time and many opportunities exist for young people—around one-fourth of these workers were sixteen to nineteen years of age, about five times the proportion for workers in all areas of employment.

Opportunities for advancement vary depending on where you work in the food service industry. Due to the relatively small size of most food serving and manufacturing establishments, opportunities for promotion are often limited. Opportunities for advancement are most often found in large restaurants, retail stores, and the military. After gaining experience, some dining room and cafeteria attendants and bartender assistants, for example, may advance to waiter, waitress, or bartender jobs. Food counter workers can advance to a variety of positions, including that of cashier, cook, food server, counter or fountain supervisor, or, for counter workers in cafeterias, to line supervisor. Some hosts and hostesses advance to supervisory jobs, such as maître d'hôtel, dining room supervisor, or restaurant manager.

Many large fast-food companies and nationwide chains operate formal management-training programs; others offer informal on-the-job training. Dependable workers who show leadership abilities may qualify for these programs. For those in the manufacturing sector of food processing, opportunities for promotion are limited to the few available supervisory or team leader positions. Those in the military will advance with time, movement up the ranks, and additional training. No matter where you work, to increase your chances of obtaining a promotion, you must demonstrate strong analytical, verbal, and people skills, as well as enthusiasm and drive.

Most entry-level workers pick up their skills on-the-job by observing and working with more experienced workers. Some employers, particularly those in fast-food restaurants, use self-instruction programs with audiovisual presentations and instructional booklets to teach new employees food preparation and service skills. Some public and private vocational schools, restaurant associations, and large restaurant chains provide classroom training in a generalized food service curriculum, but this occurs most often for food servers and bartenders. The military, however, provides plenty of training and education for those who enlist and want to become food service specialists.

Earnings

Entry-level workers typically receive an hourly wage for their work. Those in restaurants may also collect tips from customers or from a percentage of the food servers' and bartenders' earnings. Incomes vary greatly, depending on the type of job and establishment. While fast-food workers usually do not receive tips, their hourly wage rates may be higher than those of waiters and waitresses and bartenders in full-service restaurants, who typically earn more from tips than from wages. In some restaurants, workers contribute a portion of their tips to a tip pool, which is distributed among qualifying workers. Tip pools allow workers who don't usually receive tips directly from customers, such as dining room attendants, to share in the rewards of good service.

Many beginning or inexperienced workers start earning the federal minimum wage of $5.15 an hour. However, a few states set minimum wages higher than the federal minimum. Also, various minimum wage exceptions apply under specific circumstances to disabled workers, full-time students, youths under age twenty in their first ninety days of employment, and student-learners. While employers are permitted to deduct from wages the cost of any meals or lodging provided, most provide free meals and uniforms to their employees. Entry-level workers who work full-time often receive typical benefits, while part-time workers usually do not.

In some large restaurants and hotels, those who serve food and beverages and related workers belong to unions. These are the Hotel Employees and Restaurant Employees International Union (www.unitehere.org) and the Service Employees International Union (www.seiu.org). The purpose of these unions is to ensure fair compensation and safe working conditions for workers.

Dining Room Attendants

An egg-stained fork, a soiled tablecloth, or an empty saltshaker can make a customer very unhappy and can also damage a restaurant's reputation. Dining room attendants provide the quick hands and sharp eyes needed to prevent such problems from occurring. The general category of dining room attendants includes the positions of busperson, backwaiter or runner, hat and coat checker, food service assistant, host or hostess, dishwasher, and bartender's assistant or "barback." In 2002, dining room attendants occupied approximately 409,000 positions.

Dining room attendants perform many tasks that food servers would otherwise be responsible for. They clear and reset tables, carry soiled dishes to the dishwashing area, bring in trays of food, and clean up spilled food and broken dishes. By taking care of these details, attendants give waiters and waitresses more time to serve customers. In some restaurants, attendants help food servers by serving water and bread and butter to customers. Also, when business is slow, they handle various jobs such as refilling salt-and-pepper shakers and cleaning coffee pots. The following are details about each job.

Busperson

Buspersons assist the food servers in keeping clients happy and turning tables quickly. They keep water glasses filled, support waiters and waitresses in serving, and remove silverware and plates when the clientele are finished with them. They clear and reset dining tables with fresh linen and silverware when parties leave, making room for the next group of customers.

The job of busperson provides an excellent way to start acquiring food service expertise. You will gain experience working with customers and balancing dishware. You will also get a good feel for how a meal progresses and when to accomplish tasks. While busy, this is a job that requires less skill and produces less stress than that of the food servers.

Buspersons are paid an hourly wage. Nationally, the median wage for buspersons is $6.99 per hour. In some restaurants, higher-paid employees such as waiters, waitresses, and bartenders may contribute a portion of their tips to a tip pool, and buspersons may increase their earnings by receiving a portion of the tip pool. Most often, however, they receive a percentage of the food servers' tips. This is because they directly contribute to the dining experience of the clientele—for better and for worse—so it's in the busperson's best interest to make for a pleasurable experience.

Backwaiter or Runner

Backwaiters or runners serve as the liaison between the front (dining area) and back (kitchen) of the house in restaurants. They must wear more formal attire than the kitchen staff because they have to interact with patrons in the dining area. They are responsible for carrying dishes out to the tables in nicer restaurants. This helps ensure that dishes arrive to the table shortly after they are prepared.

Backwaiters or runners are paid an hourly wage for their work. It is generally in line with minimum wage, and they may receive additional compensation from the tip pool. These workers generally do not receive tips directly from customers or the food servers.

Hat and Coat Checker

Hat and coat checkers are responsible for guarding coats, hats, briefcases, and other personal articles that customers do not want in their immediate possession while dining. They typically work in a small area off the main entrance of the establishment and give patrons a ticket in exchange for their personal articles.

The hat and coat checker is paid an hourly wage for his or her work, which is typically minimum wage. Some patrons also give them tips; however, this is not to be expected. Tips generally range from $1.00 to $5.00.

Host or Hostess

Hosts and hostesses maintain reservation lists, greet customers, show guests to tables, ensure order and cleanliness in the dining area, and, in some cases, handle complaints. This job requires good organization skills, tact, a ready smile, a neat appearance, and an affinity for people. In addition, having good diplomatic skills will come in handy, as there may be tension amongst the food servers if they feel they are not getting good (high-tipping) tables. The host or hostess is often the first and last representative of the establishment that a patron sees, making this an especially important position.

Hosts and hostesses are paid an hourly wage. According to the U.S. Department of Labor, in 2002 the median hourly earnings of hosts and hostesses were $7.36. The middle 50 percent earned between $6.54 and $8.58. The lowest 10 percent earned less than $5.89, and the highest 10 percent earned more than $10.32. Wages comprised the majority of their earnings. In some cases, wages were supplemented by proceeds from tip pools. They may also receive tips directly from customers, but this is less common in this position than for the hat or coat checker. Again, tips may range from $1.00 to $5.00.

Dishwasher

Dishwashers are responsible for more than just washing dishes. They ensure that walls and floors are clean and that there is a steady supply of clean cooking equipment, utensils, dishware, and silver. Most modern food service operations have mechanical dishwashers and other machines to assist in speeding these tasks. Dishwashers are responsible for operating special machines that clean tableware quickly and efficiently. To keep machines in optimum operating order, dishwashers may have to make minor adjustments. Good sanitation and maintenance are vital to any food service operation, and dishwashers are the enforcers in this area.

In 2002 the median hourly earnings of dishwashers were $7.15. The middle 50 percent earned between $6.40 and $8.28. The lowest 10 percent earned less than $5.82, and the highest 10 percent earned more than $9.41.

Bartenders' Assistants, or Barbacks

Bartenders' assistants, or barbacks, support bartenders in maintaining bar stock, cleaning glassware, replenishing supplies of ice, and keeping the bar area neat and tidy. While barbacks are not allowed to pour or sell drinks, this job is excellent training for becoming a bartender.

Barbacks earn a combination of an hourly wage and tips from either the tip pool or from a percentage of the bartenders' tips. In 2002, median hourly earnings (including tips) of bartenders' assistants were $6.99. The middle 50 percent earned between $6.33 and $8.10. The lowest 10 percent earned less than $5.80, and the highest 10 percent earned more than $9.70. Most received over half of their earnings as wages; the rest of their income was a share of the proceeds from tip pools or bartenders' tips.

Food-Counter Workers

Counter workers serve customers in eating places that specialize in fast service and inexpensive food, such as carryout establishments, fast-food restaurants, coffee shops, diners, hospital and school cafeterias, airports, and museums, as well as other public places. Accuracy in handling orders and speed of service are the most important job skills for food-counter workers.

Duties vary depending on the work setting. Typical duties include taking customers' orders, serving food and beverages, making out checks, and taking payments. In diners, cooking, making sandwiches, preparing cold drinks, and making sundaes also are part of food-counter workers' duties.

Where food is prepared in an assembly-line manner, as in carryout establishments or school cafeterias, counter workers may take turns waiting on customers, making French fries, toasting buns, and doing other jobs preparing food. In cafeterias, counter workers serve food displayed on steam tables, carve meat, dish out vegetables, ladle sauces and soups, fill beverage glasses, and supply serving lines with desserts, salads, and other dishes. In lunchrooms and coffee shops, counter attendants take orders from customers seated at the counter, transmit orders to the kitchen, and pick up and serve food. They also fill cups with coffee, soda, and other beverages and prepare drink specialties, such as milkshakes and cappuccinos.

Counter attendants also take carryout orders from diners and wrap or place items in containers. They write itemized checks and sometimes accept payment. Usually, however, central cashiers are employed by cafeterias to take payments and make change. Some workers take orders from customers at counters or drive-through windows at fast-food restaurants. They assemble orders, hand them to customers, and accept payment. Many of these are combined food preparation and serving workers who also cook and package food, make coffee, and fill beverage cups using drink-dispensing machines. No matter what the establishment, counter workers are often responsible for keeping the establishment clean, doing jobs such as cleaning kitchen equipment, sweeping and mopping floors, and carrying out trash.

Working Conditions

Because most counter workers are on duty fewer than thirty hours a week, some work only a few to several hours a day. Some even work split shifts (for example, breakfast and dinner), so they have a few hours off in the middle of the day. This flexible schedule enables students to fit working hours around classes. For most of these workers, regardless of the setting, evening, weekend, and holiday work is often required. The exceptions to this rule are those who work in elementary, middle, and high schools; these workers have regular hours during the school week and may have summers off.

Food-counter workers must work quickly and effectively under pressure during busy periods. The ability to function as a member of a team, to stand for long periods of time, and to perform tasks within a restricted area is important in this job. Unlike food servers, food-counter workers do not handle heavy trays, but they may be exposed to the potential for minor injuries from sharp implements or flatware, wet floors, and hot utensils or grease.

Earnings

In 2002 the median hourly earnings of combined food preparation and serving workers, including fast-food, were $6.97. The middle 50 percent earned between $6.23 and $8.08. The lowest 10 percent earned less than $5.74, and the highest 10 percent earned more than $9.33. Although some combined food preparation and serving workers receive a part of their earnings as tips, fast-food workers usually do not.

Median hourly earnings of counter attendants in cafeterias, food concessions, and coffee shops were $7.32 in 2002. The middle 50 percent earned between $6.52 and $8.53 an hour. The lowest 10 percent earned less than $5.87, and the highest 10 percent earned more than $10.39.

While tips may reach the national average of between 10 and 20 percent of patrons' checks, most often for these positions, tips are collected in a jar on the counter and are generally lower than the national average. In addition to their pay, many counter workers receive free meals at work and may be furnished with uniforms.

Food Preparation Workers

Food preparation workers can be found in a variety of settings, including restaurants, kitchens, and even manufacturing plants. In fact, there are approximately 850,000 food preparation workers on the job today. These workers prepare, season, and cook a wide variety of foods—from soups, snacks, and salads to entrees, side dishes, and desserts. They work under the direction of chefs and cooks who create recipes and prepare meals, while the food preparation workers peel and cut vegetables, trim meat, prepare poultry, and perform other duties such as keeping work areas clean and monitoring temperatures of ovens and stovetops. In restaurants, these workers are often referred to as line or prep cooks. Grocery and specialty food stores employ chefs, cooks, and food preparation workers to develop recipes and prepare meals to go. Typically, entrees, side dishes, salads, or other items are prepared in large quantities and stored at an appropriate temperature until they are to be served.

Food preparation workers perform many routine and repetitive tasks, such as readying ingredients for complex dishes, slicing and dicing vegetables, and composing salads and cold items under the direction of chefs and cooks. They weigh and measure ingredients, assemble the necessary pots and pans, and stir and strain soups and sauces. Food preparation workers may cut and grind meats, poultry, and seafood in preparation for cooking. Their responsibilities also include cleaning work areas, equipment, utensils, dishes, and silverware.

In terms of advancement, many food preparation workers move into assistant or line cook positions. From there, with additional classroom or on-the-job training, they may be able to attain a cook position.

Working Conditions

The kitchen is almost always a dynamic and fast-paced environment in which to work, although conditions vary considerably depending on the environment. Kitchen staffs in restaurants invariably work in small quarters against hot stoves and ovens. They are under constant pressure to prepare meals quickly, while ensuring quality is maintained and safety and sanitation guidelines are observed. Working conditions vary with the type and quantity of food prepared and the local laws governing food service operations. Workers usually must withstand the pressure and strain of standing for hours at a time, lifting heavy pots and kettles, and working near hot ovens and grills. Job hazards include slips and falls, cuts, and burns, but injuries are seldom serious.

The wide range in dining hours and variety of food service operations creates plenty of work opportunities for individuals who are seeking supplemental income, flexible work hours, or variable schedules, as well as for those who want regular hours and a forty-hour workweek. For example, almost 20 percent of cooks and food preparation workers were sixteen to nineteen years of age in 2002, and almost 10 percent had variable schedules. Kitchen workers employed by schools may work during the school year only, usually for nine or ten months.

Earnings

While the earnings for food preparation and related workers vary according to the nature of the place in which they work, in 2002 the median hourly earnings of food preparation workers were $7.85. The middle 50 percent earned between $6.72 and $9.43, the lowest 10 percent earned less than $5.96, and the highest 10 percent earned more than $11.37. Median hourly earnings in the industries employing the largest number of food preparation workers were:

Elementary and secondary schools	$8.74
Grocery stores	$8.43
Nursing care facilities	$7.94
Full-service restaurants	$7.66
Limited-service eating places	$7.07

In 2002 the median hourly earnings of short-order cooks were $7.82. The middle 50 percent earned between $6.69 and $9.59, the lowest 10 percent earned less than $5.93, and the highest 10 percent earned more than $11.25. Median hourly earnings in the industries employing the largest number of short-order cooks were:

Full-service restaurants	$8.29
Taverns and bars	$7.85
Other amusement and recreation industries	$7.74
Gasoline stations	$7.04
Limited-service eating places	$6.97

Finally, in 2002 the median hourly earnings of fast-food cooks were $6.90. The middle 50 percent earned between $6.16 and $8.03, the lowest 10 percent earned less than $5.68, and the highest 10 percent earned more than $9.13.

Additionally, some employers provide employees with uniforms and free meals, but federal law permits employers to deduct from their employees' wages the cost or fair value of any meals or lodging provided, and some employers do so. Food preparation workers who work full-time often receive typical benefits, but part-time workers usually do not.

Food Processing Occupations

Food processing occupations include many different types of workers who process raw food products into the finished goods sold by grocers or wholesalers, restaurants, or institutional food services, including baked goods, highly refined foods, and meat products. These workers perform a variety of tasks and are responsible for producing many of the food products found in every household and on the grocery shelves.

Bakers in a food processing operation mix and bake ingredients in accordance with recipes to produce varying quantities of breads, pastries, and other baked goods. Bakers commonly are employed in grocery stores and specialty shops and produce breads, pastries, and other baked goods for consumption on the premises or for sale as specialty baked goods. In manufacturing, bakers produce goods in large quantities, using high-volume mixing machines, ovens, and other equipment. Goods produced in large quantities usually are available for sale through distributors, grocery stores, or manufacturers' outlets.

Others in food processing occupations include food batch makers, who set up and operate equipment that mixes, blends, or cooks ingredients used in the manufacture of food products according to formulas or recipes; food cooking-machine operators and tenders, who operate or tend cooking equipment such as steam cooking vats, deep-fry cookers, pressure cookers, kettles, and boilers to prepare food products such as meat, sugar, cheese, and grain; and food and tobacco roasting, baking, and drying machine operators and tenders, who use equipment to reduce the moisture content of food or tobacco products or to process food in preparation for canning. Some of the machines that are used include hearth ovens, kiln driers, roasters, char kilns, steam ovens, and vacuum drying equipment.

Meat, poultry, and fish cutters and trimmers are employed at different stages in the process by which animal carcasses are converted into manageable pieces of meat, known as boxed meat, that are suitable for sale to wholesalers and retailers. They also prepare ready-to-heat foods. This often entails filleting meat or fish or cutting it into bite-sized pieces, preparing and adding vegetables, or applying sauces, marinades, or breading. Many of these workers are found in animal slaughtering and processing plants, while butchers and meat cutters usually are employed at the retail level. As a result, the nature of these jobs varies significantly. Meat cutters and butchers require some training prior to getting the job, so they are featured in the following chapter on middle-level positions.

In animal slaughtering and processing plants, cattle, hogs, goats, and sheep carcasses are cut into large wholesale pieces, such as rounds, loins, ribs, and chucks, to facilitate the handling, distribution, and marketing of meat. Workers in these plants also produce hamburger meat and meat trimmings, which are used to prepare sausages, luncheon meats, and other meat products. Meat processors usually work on assembly lines, with each individual responsible for only a few of the many cuts produced by the plant. Depending on the type of cut, they use knives, cleavers, meat saws, band saws, or other, often dangerous, equipment.

Working Conditions

According to the U.S. Department of Labor, food processing workers held 625,000 jobs in 2002. Employment among the various types of food processing occupations was distributed as follows:

Bakers	173,000
Meat, poultry, and fish cutters and trimmers	154,000
Meat packers	128,000

Food batch makers	74,000
Food cooking-machine operators	34,000
Roasting, baking, and drying machine operators	19,000
All other food processing workers	42,000

About 36 percent of all food processing workers were employed in animal processing plants. Another 21 percent were employed at grocery stores. Most of the remainder worked in food manufacturing. Food processing jobs are generally concentrated in communities with food processing plants.

Working conditions vary by type and size of establishment. Food batch makers; roasting, baking, and drying machine operators; and food cooking-machine operators typically work in production areas that are specially designed for food preservation or processing. Food batch makers, in particular, work in kitchen-type, assembly-line production facilities. Because this work involves food, work areas must meet governmental sanitary regulations. The ovens, as well as the motors of blenders, mixers, and other equipment, often make work areas very warm and noisy. There are some hazards, such as burns, created by the equipment that these workers use. These workers spend a great deal of time on their feet and generally work a regular forty-hour week that may include evening and night shifts.

In animal processing plants and large retail food establishments, workers spend much of their day in large meat cutting rooms equipped with power machines and conveyors. In small retail markets, the butcher or fish cleaner may work in a cramped space behind the meat or fish counter. To prevent viral and bacterial infections, work areas must be kept clean and sanitary.

Meat, poultry, and fish cutters and trimmers often work in cold, damp rooms that are refrigerated to prevent meat from spoiling; they are damp because meat cutting generates large amounts of blood, condensation, and fat. Cool, damp floors increase the likelihood of slips and falls. In addition, cool temperatures, long periods of standing, and repetitious physical tasks make the work tiring. As a result, these workers are often more susceptible to injury than are most other workers. In fact, meatpacking plants had one of the highest incidences of work-related injury and illness of any industry in 2002. Nearly one in seven employees in such plants experienced a work-related injury or illness that year.

Injuries include cuts and occasional amputations, which occur when knives, cleavers, or power tools are used improperly. Also, repetitive slicing and lifting often lead to cumulative trauma injuries, such as carpal tunnel syndrome. To reduce the incidence of cumulative trauma injuries, some employers have reduced employee workloads, added prescribed rest periods, redesigned jobs and tools, and promoted increased awareness of early warning signs so that steps can be taken to prevent further injury. Nevertheless, workers in the occupation still face the serious threat of disabling injuries.

Earnings

Median annual earnings of food batch makers in 2002 were $21,920. The middle 50 percent earned between $16,720 and $28,740, the lowest 10 percent earned less than $13,930, and the highest 10 percent earned more than $35,110. Median annual earnings in the industries employing the largest numbers of food batch makers are as follows:

Dairy product manufacturing	$26,330
Fruit and vegetable preserving and specialty food manufacturing	$22,980
Other food manufacturing	$22,850

| Bakeries and tortilla manufacturing | $22,530 |
| Sugar and confectionary product manufacturing | $21,390 |

Median annual earnings for food cooking-machine operators were $21,860 in 2002. The middle 50 percent earned between $16,900 and $28,160, the lowest 10 percent earned less than $14,380, and the highest 10 percent earned more than $34,890. Median annual earnings in fruit and vegetable preserving and specialty food manufacturing, the industry employing the largest number of food cooking-machine operators, were $25,320 in 2002.

In 2002, median annual earnings for roasting, baking, and drying machine operators and tenders were $23,260, and for all other food processing workers, $19,410.

Meat, poultry, and fish cutters and trimmers typically earn less than butchers and meat cutters, who are discussed in the following chapter. In 2002, median annual earnings for these lower-skilled workers were $17,820. The middle 50 percent earned between $15,800 and $21,170, the lowest 10 percent earned less than $14,270, and the highest 10 percent earned more than $24,840. Median annual earnings in the industries employing the largest numbers of meat, poultry, and fish cutters and trimmers are as follows:

Grocery stores	$20,900
Grocery and related product wholesalers	$18,440
Animal processing	$17,710
Seafood product preparation and packaging	$15,660

Food processing workers generally receive typical benefits, including pension plans for union members or those employed by grocery stores. However, poultry workers rarely earn substantial benefits. In 2002, 25 percent of all butchers and other meat, poultry, and fish processing workers were union members or were covered by a union contract. Sixteen percent of all bakers and 18 percent of all food batch makers also were union members or were covered by a union contract. Many food processing workers are members of the United Food and Commercial Workers International Union (www.ufcw.org).

Military Food Service Specialists

More than one million nutritious and well-balanced meals are prepared each day by trained staff in military kitchens. Depending on the size of the military contingent being served, some kitchens prepare thousands of meals at one time, while others prepare food for only a few people at each sitting. Food service specialists prepare a variety of different foods according to standard and dietetic recipes. In addition, these workers order and inspect food supplies and prepare meats for cooking—and they are members of a military branch. All five branches of the military—U.S. Army, Navy, Air Force, Marines, and Coast Guard—offer jobs in this position for enlisted personnel.

Military food service specialists wear many hats in addition to that of their standard issue uniform. These workers order, receive, and inspect food products; prepare cuts of meat and vegetables using a variety of instruments; cook, bake, and fry a range of foods; serve food in various settings, including dining halls, hospitals, field kitchens, or aboard ships; and clean their workspaces in the kitchen and dining areas.

For those assigned to military food service positions, typical job training consists of two to three months of classroom instruction, which includes hands-on food preparation instruction. Classroom content typically includes preparing standard and dietetic menus and recipes; cooking various foodstuffs and bakery products; ordering and stocking food and supplies; and properly storing perishable items, such as beef, chicken, and fish. Additional information on terms of enlistment and education and training in the military is described in Chapter 8.

Working Conditions

Military personnel are stationed throughout the United States and in many countries around the world. More than half of all military jobs are located in California, Texas, North Carolina, Virginia, Florida, and Georgia. About 395,000 individuals were stationed outside the United States in 2002, including those assigned to ships at sea. Approximately 104,000 of these were stationed in Europe, mainly in Germany, and another 85,000 were assigned to East Asia and the Pacific area, mostly in Japan and the Republic of Korea.

The services have about twenty-eight thousand food service specialists. Each year, they need new specialists due to changes in personnel and the demands of the field. After job training, food service specialists help prepare and serve food under close supervision. Some food service specialists work as bakers, cooks, butchers, or meat cutters. With experience, they work more independently and may train new food service specialists. Eventually, they may become head cooks, chefs, or food service supervisors.

Food service specialists normally work in clean, sanitary kitchens and dining facilities. They may sometimes work in refrigerated meat lockers. They also may work outdoors in tents while preparing and serving food under field conditions. Food service specialists may have to lift and carry heavy containers of foodstuffs and large cooking utensils.

Earnings

The enlistment contract obligates the military to provide the agreed-upon job, rating, pay, cash bonuses for enlistment in certain occupations, medical and other benefits, occupational training, and continuing education. In addition, the military offers tuition assistance in both military and civilian colleges in return for service—enlisted personnel must serve satisfactorily for the period specified.

The most important components of compensation in the military are pay and allowances. There are various types of pay. Basic pay is the fundamental component of military pay; all members receive it and typically it is the largest component of a member's pay. A grade (usually the same as rank) and the number of years of service determine the amount of basic pay a member of the military receives. Most new members start out at grade E-1, which means that their pay is approximately $1,064 to $1,150 per month for the first year of service. Visit the U.S. Department of Labor, Bureau of Labor Statistics at www.bls.gov for additional information on military pay.

In addition to receiving basic pay, military personnel are provided with free room and board (or a tax-free housing and subsistence allowance), free medical and dental care, a military clothing allowance, military supermarket and department store shopping privileges, thirty days of paid vacation a year (referred to as leave), and travel opportunities. In many duty stations, military personnel may receive a housing allowance that can be used for off-base housing. This allowance can be substantial, but it varies greatly by rank and duty station. Most allowances are not taxable, which is an additional benefit of military pay.

Employment Outlook

The overwhelming majority of the entry-level jobs featured in this chapter can be found in restaurants, coffee shops, and bars. Additional places of employment include hotels, amusement parks, casinos, schools, grocery stores, hospitals and nursing homes, and golf and country clubs. Jobs are located throughout the country, but they are typically plentiful in large cities and tourist areas. Other interesting options include vacation resorts and spas, which tend to offer seasonal employment. In fact, some adventurous workers alternate between summer and winter resorts, instead of remaining in one area the entire year.

Job openings for dining room attendants, food-counter workers, and food preparation workers alike are expected to be plentiful in the coming years. Many openings will come about from the need to replace workers who find jobs in other occupations. Among part-time workers, turnover is particularly high. This is because approximately 50 percent of dining room attendants are students who work part-time while attending school.

Employment growth will provide additional openings. Jobs are expected to increase faster than the average for all occupations through the year 2006, as population growth and higher incomes create more business for food service establishments. The continuing fast-paced lifestyle of many Americans and the addition of healthier foods at many fast-food restaurants are contributing to the expansion of the restaurant industry, which will create many job openings. Therefore, jobs should be relatively plentiful and easy to find. That said, employment of some kinds of dining room attendants, food preparation workers, and dishwashers will grow more slowly than other food and beverage serving and related workers, because diners increasingly are eating at more casual dining spots, such as coffee bars and sandwich shops, rather than at the full-service restaurants that employ more of these workers.

For those working in food processing occupations, increasingly cheaper meat imports from abroad will have a negative effect on domestic employment for those working with meat products. For all food processing occupations, job growth will be concentrated at the manufacturing level, as more food preparation shifts from retail stores to food processing plants. Nevertheless, job opportunities should be available at all levels of the occupation due to the need to replace experienced workers who transfer to other occupations or leave the labor force.

Working in the military is about as stable as a job gets in terms of receiving a regular paycheck. That said, there is plenty of uncertainty about where you will be stationed, when you will have to move, and where you will have to work during times of both peace and war. These are all things you'll need to carefully consider before making your career choice.

4

MIDDLE-LEVEL POSITIONS

SUCCEEDING IN THE food service industry takes drive, ambition, and the desire to please people. After all, the success of the industry is built on customer service. It also requires an energetic, outgoing personality and the ability to be comfortable working with people from a range of backgrounds. You also need to be a quick thinker and have the ability to solve problems immediately.

This chapter covers middle-level positions in the food service industry. These jobs generally require some previous direct or indirect experience in the field. On-the-job training for a few days to a week is usually provided for the recently hired, but the best jobs will be ones you can attain only if you have done prior work in a similar establishment.

Food Servers

Food servers, commonly known as waiters and waitresses, are responsible for taking food orders and providing service to customers. Those working as food servers must like people and be poised and efficient under the stress of simultaneous demands. Many energetic, outgoing people make this their career.

All food servers, whether they work in small lunchrooms or fashionable restaurants, have essentially the same job. Food servers take customers' orders, serve food and beverages, and deliver bills to the tables. However, the way in which food servers perform their duties may vary considerably. In coffee shops serving routine, straightforward fare, such as salads, soups, and sandwiches, food servers are expected to provide fast, efficient, and courteous service. In fine dining restaurants, where more complicated meals are prepared and often served over several courses, waiters and waitresses provide more formal service emphasizing personal, attentive treatment and a more leisurely pace. They may recommend certain dishes and identify ingredients or explain how various items on the menu are made. Some prepare salads, desserts, or other menu items tableside, and they may recommend wines to pair with food if the establishment doesn't employ a sommelier. All food servers are responsible for checking the identification of patrons to ensure they meet the minimum age requirement for the purchase of alcoholic beverages.

Some food servers perform duties other than waiting on tables. These additional tasks may include setting up tables and clearing and carrying soiled flatware to the kitchen. This typically occurs in more informal, family-style restaurants. Only very small restaurants combine waiting on tables with counter service or working the cash register; larger or more formal restaurants frequently relieve their food servers of these additional duties.

This type of job is listed as a middle-level position primarily because, depending on the establishment, you may need to have some kind of relevant work experience. This is especially true in the more upscale restaurants, spas, and resorts. For these types of establishments, you'll need to have fairly extensive experience working in increasingly prestigious places. For the more casual environments, you may not need direct experience working as a food server. For example, in pubs that also serve food, you may be hired as a food server even though your previous experience was as a host or hostess. Some family-style chain restaurants may even hire you without your having any pertinent restaurant experience at all.

Working Conditions

Approximately two million food servers are employed in the United States today. The majority of them are employed in restaurants, although some also work in hotels, colleges, and airports that have sit-down restaurant facilities. Seasonal employment can be found in vacation resorts and spas. Similar to those jobs described in the previous chapter, jobs for food servers are located throughout the country but are most plentiful in large cities and tourist areas.

The hours food servers work vary depending on the establishment. Some places are only open for lunch, while others only serve food during the evening. In settings like cruise ships or resorts, servers may work longer hours covering several shifts. Regardless, most food servers are required to work on holidays and weekends. The wide range in dining and, thus, working hours makes this job good for those who need flexible, part-time work. In fact, nearly half of all servers work part-time.

As is true of most jobs in the restaurant division of the food service industry, this job entails standing for long periods of time and often carrying heavy trays of food, dishes, and glassware. During busy dining periods, food servers are under pressure to serve customers quickly and efficiently. Overall, the work is relatively safe, but servers must take care to avoid slips, falls, and burns.

Training, Other Qualifications, and Advancement

An applicant who has had at least two or three years of high school and some experience is most preferred by employers. A person may start as a food server or advance to that position after working as a host or hostess or food counter worker. Although most food servers obtain their skills through on-the-job training, at least three months' experience is preferred by larger restaurants and hotels. Some private and public vocational schools, restaurant associations, and large restaurant chains provide classroom training. Other employers use self-instruction programs to train new employees. In these programs, a worker learns food preparation and service skills by watching instructional DVDs and videos and reading booklets on the subject.

Close and constant contact with the public makes a neat appearance and even disposition important qualifications for this occupation. Physical stamina is also important because this is a very physically demanding job. Food servers should have good mathematical skills. In restaurants specializing in foreign foods where some patrons may not speak English, knowledge of a foreign language is helpful. Successful food servers are those who genuinely like people, offer good service, and possess the ability to sell foods and upgrade beverage choices rather than just take orders. Advancement can be to supervisory jobs, such as maître d'hôtel or dining room supervisor. Some supervisory workers advance to jobs as restaurant managers.

Earnings

According to the Department of Labor, in 2002, median hourly earnings (including tips) of food servers were $6.80. The middle

50 percent earned between $6.13 and $8.00. The lowest 10 percent earned less than $5.70, and the highest 10 percent earned more than $11.00.

For most food servers, higher earnings are primarily the result of receiving more in tips rather than higher hourly wages; tips usually average between 10 and 20 percent of guests' checks. Food servers working in busy, expensive restaurants earn the most because a customer's total tab will be substantially higher than that of a less expensive restaurant. Food servers are often required to give a portion of their tips to the bartender for providing them with drinks quickly and to buspersons for helping them turn tables. As stated, food servers receive an hourly wage in addition to tips. This sum is often less than the minimum wage. In fact, employers are only obligated to pay at least $2.13 an hour in direct wages. In addition to monetary compensation, most food servers receive meals at work and some are furnished with uniforms.

The principal union organizing food servers is the Hotel and Restaurant Employees and Bartenders International Union.

Employment Outlook

In the years ahead, job opportunities are expected to be plentiful. This is mainly due to the need to replace the food servers because of high turnover rates. Approximately 25 percent of the food servers are students, most of whom work part-time while attending school and then find other jobs after graduation. Many job openings also will result from employment growth. The best employment opportunities for beginning food servers will be found in the thousands of informal restaurants. Those seeking jobs in expensive restaurants may find keen competition for the jobs that become available.

Bartenders

A bartender's career offers excellent opportunities to meet people while working in many different types of establishments. The duties of a bartender encompass both the preparation and service aspects of a food service operation. Bartenders serve customers at the bar and fill drink orders taken by food servers. A congenial personality and the knowledge of ordering for and stocking the bar, as well as maintaining inventories of liquor and glassware, are needed to excel at this job. In addition, bartenders must be familiar with state and local laws concerning the sale of alcoholic beverages. Both the bartender and his or her employer can be fined for serving alcohol to minors.

A bartender is a master of mixology. Cosmopolitans, martinis, and manhattans are merely a few of the cocktails represented in the art of mixology, or bartending. By combining, in exact proportion, ingredients selected from a variety of liquors, spirits, and mixes, bartenders can create wild concoctions to please and delight their customers. A well-stocked bar contains many types and brands of liquor and soft drinks, fruit juices, cream, soda, and tonic water. Also, bartenders serve beer, wine, and a variety of nonalcoholic beverages.

Some people prefer their cocktails a certain way, so bartenders are often asked to mix drinks to suit a customer's particular taste. Most bartenders are required to know hundreds of drink recipes and be capable of mixing drinks accurately by sight alone in order to serve drinks quickly and without wasting anything, even during the busiest periods. In addition to mixing and serving drinks, bartenders may be called upon to serve limited food items or snacks to customers seated at the bar, collect payment, operate the cash register, and clean up when customers leave. While many large operations are now using equipment that mixes drinks automatically, bartenders still must be efficient and knowledgeable to handle unusual orders and to work when the automatic equipment is not functioning.

Working Conditions

In 2002, there were 463,000 bartenders employed in the United States. While most worked in restaurants and bars, others were employed in hotels and private clubs. Approximately 10 percent were self-employed, which means they owned the bar at which they worked. Several thousand people, many of whom also work in other occupations or attend college, tend bar part-time. Often they serve at banquets and private parties, which are held at restaurants, hotels, or even private homes. The majority of bartenders work in urban population centers, but many are also employed in small communities. Seasonal employment is available at vacation resorts, as well.

Working conditions vary depending on the place of employment. Bartenders may work more than forty hours per week, and night work, weekend work, and split shifts are common. For many bartenders, the opportunity for friendly conversation with customers and the possibility of some day managing or owning a bar or restaurant of their own offsets these disadvantages. For others, the opportunity to get part-time employment is important. You should keep in mind that some state and local regulations require that a bartender be at least twenty-one years of age. In addition, because a bartender stands for many hours, good physical condition is necessary. Better than average strength is sometimes needed to lift heavy cases of liquors or mixes.

Training, Other Qualifications, and Advancement

Because bartenders play a significant role in making an establishment attractive to customers, a pleasant and outgoing personality is a must for this career. In addition to understanding and liking all kinds of people, a bartender must have an excellent memory for faces, names, and recipes. Many bartenders pride themselves on being able to fill any drink order without looking up a recipe, and they are able to mix and serve drinks with flair, a quality that helps make them popular with customers and employers alike. A good bartender must be able to work accurately and rapidly, often mixing drinks by eye alone. Busy periods in popular operations can create considerable pressure, making a cool efficiency, coupled with attention to detail, an occupational necessity.

Most bartenders learn their trade on-the-job. While preparing drinks at home can be good practice, it does not qualify a person to be a bartender. People who wish to become bartenders can get valuable experience by working as bartenders' assistants or barbacks, dining room attendants, or food servers. In addition, some bartenders acquire their skills by attending a bartending or vocational and technical school. These programs often include instruction on state and local laws and regulations, cocktail recipes, attire and conduct, and stocking a bar. Some of these schools help their graduates find jobs. Although few employers require any minimum level of educational attainment, some specialized training is usually needed in food handling and legal issues surrounding serving alcoholic beverages and tobacco. Employers are more likely to hire and promote based on people skills and personal qualities rather than education.

Neighborhood bars, small restaurants, and resorts usually offer a beginner the best entry opportunities. After acquiring experience, a bartender may wish to work in a large restaurant or cocktail lounge, where salaries are higher and promotion opportunities are greater. Promotional opportunities in this field are limited; however, it is possible to advance to head bartender, wine steward, or beverage manager. Some bartenders go on to open their own businesses. To own and operate a tavern or bar, bartenders must excel at keeping their own business records and hiring, training, and directing staff.

Earnings

Bartenders had median hourly earnings (including tips) of $7.21 in 2002. The middle 50 percent earned between $6.33 and $9.02. The lowest 10 percent earned less than $5.76, and the highest 10 percent earned more than $11.96. Like food servers, bartenders employed in public bars may receive more than half of their earnings as tips, but they generally make more than food servers. Bartenders collect a portion of the food servers' tips and they give their barbacks a portion of theirs. Service bartenders often are paid higher hourly wages to offset their lower tip earnings. Often bartenders receive free meals at work and may be given bar jackets or complete uniforms.

Employment Outlook

Through the year 2006, employment of bartenders is expected to increase about as fast as the average for all occupations. Like most occupations in the restaurant industry, job turnover is high, so there are generally always positions available. That said, when the economy suffers, fewer people dine out in fine dining establishments, which may cause these restaurants to go out of business, thus affecting the prospects for those interested in working in such places. Bars and taverns, however, are less likely to feel the economy's effects.

Cooks and Chefs

A reputation for serving fine food is an asset to any restaurant, whether it prides itself on home cooking or exotic cuisine. Cooks and chefs are largely responsible for the reputation a restaurant acquires. Many have earned fame for both themselves and the restaurants or hotels where they work because of their skill in creating new dishes and improving on familiar ones. Cooks and chefs are the artists and administrators of the food service industry, and some of the most interesting jobs in the entire industry belong to them. There is a strong demand for talented, well-trained cooks and chefs all over the country and many prestigious schools available to train them.

Although the terms chef and cook are often used interchangeably, the professional chef is generally a far more skilled, trained, and experienced person. Chefs, sometimes referred to as head cooks, coordinate the work of the kitchen staff and often direct certain kinds of food preparation. They decide the size of the serving, plan menus, and buy food supplies.

The positions of chef and cook are both highly creative ones. In large operations, the positions are often specialized with one or more individuals responsible for specific product categories such as vegetables, soups, meats, or sauces. For example, the pastry chef is responsible for the desserts. This includes baking cakes, cookies, pies, breads, and rolls, and sometimes skill in cake decoration is also required.

Smaller restaurants usually feature a limited number of easy-to-prepare, short-order specialties and ready-made desserts from a nearby bakery. Usually, one cook prepares all the food with the help of a short-order cook and one or two kitchen helpers. Here the cook, in addition to food preparation, may be responsible for purchasing foodstuffs and supplies, planning menus, and supervising kitchen staff.

In large eating establishments, which usually have more varied menus and prepare more of the food they serve, the chef or executive chef is usually in charge of everybody and everything involved in the preparation process. The chef is responsible for techniques, supplies, and, to a great extent, profits. Supervisory responsibilities may include directing several cooks and a large staff of helpers and assistants. The chef also may be called upon to develop new recipes.

Job duties vary depending on the kind of cook or chef. For each meal, institution and cafeteria cooks prepare a large quantity of a limited number of entrees, vegetables, and desserts. Restaurant cooks usually prepare a wider selection of dishes, cooking most orders individually. Short-order cooks prepare foods in restaurants and coffee shops that emphasize fast service and quick food preparation. They grill and garnish hamburgers, prepare sandwiches, fry eggs, and cook French fries, often working on several orders at the same time. Fast-food cooks prepare a limited selection of menu items in fast-food restaurants. They cook and package batches of food, such as hamburgers and fried chicken, to be kept warm until served. Private household cooks plan and prepare meals in private homes according to the client's tastes or dietary needs. They order groceries and supplies, clean the kitchen, and wash dishes and utensils. They also may serve meals.

Working Conditions

Working conditions vary by organization and location. Many kitchens have modern equipment, convenient work areas, and air-conditioning. But others, particularly older and smaller eating places, are frequently marginally equipped and poorly ventilated. Some safety hazards include cooking heat and sharp implements, but good safety standards have reduced accident risks in most organizations. Other variations in working conditions depend on the type and quantity of food being prepared and local laws governing food service operations. In the majority of kitchens, however, cooks stand most of the time, lift heavy pots and kettles, and work near hot ovens and ranges.

Cooks and chefs are often called upon to work holidays, late evenings, and weekends in restaurants. However, work hours in offices, factories, or other food service institutions might be more regular. Cooks employed in public and private schools usually work during the school year only, normally for nine to ten months. The distribution of the number of jobs among the various types of chefs and cooks is as follows:

Cooks, restaurant	727,000
Cooks, fast-food	588,000
Cooks, institution and cafeteria	436,000
Cooks, short-order	227,000
Chefs and head cooks	132,000
Cooks, private household	8,000

More than three-fifths of all chefs and cooks are employed in restaurants and other food services and drinking places. Nearly one-fifth work in institutions such as schools, universities, hospitals, and nursing care facilities. Grocery stores, hotels, gasoline stations with convenience stores, and other organizations employ the remainder. Indeed, jobs are available almost everywhere food is prepared for consumption outside the home, including department stores, airports, government agencies, factories, private clubs, and steamships.

Training, Other Qualifications, and Advancement

A high school diploma and, oftentimes, more advanced training is recommended for those planning a career as a cook or chef. High school or vocational school programs offer courses in basic food safety and handling procedures and general business and computer classes for those who want to manage or open their own place. Many school districts, in cooperation with state departments of education, provide on-the-job training and summer workshops for cafeteria kitchen workers who aspire to become cooks. Large corporations in the food services and hospitality industries also offer paid internships and summer jobs to those just starting out in the field. Finally, don't overlook internships, which provide valuable experience and can lead to placement in more formal chef-training programs.

Executive chefs and head cooks who work in fine restaurants require many years of training and experience, as well as an intense desire to cook. Some chefs and cooks start their training in high school or post–high school vocational programs, while others receive formal training through independent cooking schools, professional culinary institutes, or two- or four-year college degree programs in the hospitality or culinary arts. In addition, some large hotels and restaurants operate their own training and job-placement programs for chefs and cooks. Regardless, most formal training programs require some form of apprenticeship, internship, or outplacement program with an affiliated restaurant. Professional culinary institutes, industry associations, and trade unions also sponsor formal apprenticeship programs in coordination with the U.S. Department of Labor. Additionally, chefs are trained on-the-job, receiving real work experience and training from chef mentors in the restaurants where they work.

People who have had courses in commercial food preparation may start in a cook or chef job without spending a lot of time in lower-skilled kitchen jobs. Their education may give them an advantage when looking for jobs in better restaurants. Some vocational programs in high schools offer training, but employers usually prefer training given by trade schools, vocational centers, colleges, professional associations, or trade unions. Postsecondary courses range from a few months to two years or more, and degree-granting programs are open only to high school graduates.

Chefs also may compete and test for certification as master chefs. Although certification is not required to enter the field, it can be a measure of accomplishment and lead to further advancement and higher-paying positions. The armed forces are another good source of training and experience that you shouldn't overlook.

Although curricula vary, students in formal culinary training programs spend most of their time in kitchens learning to use the appropriate equipment and to prepare meals through actual practice. They learn good knife techniques, safe food-handling procedures, and proper use and care of kitchen equipment. Training programs often include courses in nutrition, menu planning, portion control, purchasing and inventory methods, proper food storage procedures, and use of leftover food to minimize waste.

Students also learn sanitation and public health rules for handling food. Classes in food service management, computer accounting and inventory software, and banquet service are featured in some training programs. Vocational or trade-school programs typically offer more basic training in preparing food, such as food handling and sanitation procedures, nutrition, slicing and dicing methods for various kinds of meats and vegetables, and basic cooking methods, such as baking, broiling, and grilling.

The number of formal and informal culinary training programs continues to increase to meet demand. Formal programs, which offer education leading to a certificate or a two- or four-year degree, are geared more for training chefs for fine-dining or upscale restaurants. They offer a wider array of options and specialties, such as advanced cooking techniques or foods and variety of cooking styles from around the world. The American Culinary Federation (www.acfchefs.org) accredits more than one hundred formal training programs and sponsors apprenticeship programs around the country. Typical apprenticeships last three years and combine classroom training and work experience. Accreditation is an indication that a culinary program meets recognized standards regarding course content, facilities, and quality of instruction. The American Culinary Federation also certifies pastry professionals and culinary educators in addition to various levels of chefs. Certification standards are based primarily on experience and formal training. (See Culinary Arts Schools Worldwide at www.culinaryprograms.com for more information.)

Important characteristics for chefs and cooks include working well as part of a team, having a keen sense of taste and smell, and working efficiently to turn out meals rapidly. Personal cleanliness is essential. In addition, the knowledge of a foreign language may improve communication with other restaurant staff, vendors, and the restaurant's clientele.

Advancement opportunities for chefs and cooks are better than for most other food service occupations. Advancement opportunities depend on the individual's training, work experience, and ability to perform more responsible and sophisticated tasks. Chefs and cooks who demonstrate an eagerness to learn new cooking skills and to accept greater responsibility may move up within the kitchen and take on responsibility for training or supervising newer or lesser-skilled kitchen staff. Many cooks acquire high paying positions and new cooking skills by moving from one operation to another. Others gradually advance to chef positions or supervisory or management positions, particularly in hotels, clubs, or the larger, more elegant restaurants. Some eventually enter business as caterers or restaurant owners; others may become instructors in vocational programs in high schools, junior and community colleges, and other academic institutions.

Earnings

Wages of chefs and cooks vary greatly according to region of the country and the type of food services establishment in which they work. Wages usually are highest in elegant restaurants and hotels, where many executive chefs are employed, and in major metropolitan areas. In 2002 the median hourly earnings of chefs and head cooks were $13.43. The middle 50 percent earned between $9.86 and $19.03, the lowest 10 percent earned less than $7.66, and the highest 10 percent earned more than $25.86. The median hourly earnings of restaurant cooks were $9.16. The middle 50 percent earned between $7.64 and $10.93, the lowest 10 percent earned less than $6.58, and the highest 10 percent earned more than $13.21. Finally, the median hourly earnings of institution and cafeteria cooks were $8.72. The middle 50 percent earned between $7.06 and $10.83, the lowest 10 percent earned less than $6.10, and the highest 10 percent earned more than $13.34. Keep in mind that highly reputable chefs will earn substantially more.

In some large hotels and restaurants, kitchen workers belong to unions. The principal unions are the Hotel Employees and Restaurant Employees International Union and the Service Employees International Union.

Employment Outlook

In general, employment of cooks and chefs is expected to increase faster than the average for all occupations through the year 2006. However, projected employment growth varies by specialty. The number of higher-skilled chefs and cooks working in full-service restaurants—those that offer table service and more varied menus—is expected to increase about as fast as the average. Much of the increase in this segment will come from more casual rather than upscale full-service restaurants.

Dining trends suggest increasing numbers of meals eaten away from home, growth in family dining restaurants, and greater limits on expense-account meals. Employment of institution and cafeteria chefs and cooks will show little or no growth. Their employment will not keep pace with the rapid growth in the educational and health services industries, where their employment is concentrated. Offices, schools, and hospitals increasingly contract out their food services in an effort to make institutional food more attractive to their workers, students, staff, visitors, and patients. Many of the contracted food service companies emphasize simple menu items and employ short-order cooks instead of institution and cafeteria cooks, thus reducing the demand for these workers. Employment of chefs and cooks who prepare meals-to-go, such as those who work in the prepared foods sections of grocery or specialty food stores, should increase faster than the average as people continue to demand quality meals and convenience.

Maître d's

Perhaps more than any other person in the restaurant (with maybe the exception of the chef), the maître d' is the face and representative of the establishment. A maître d' is often the first and last person a customer sees and thus can make or break a dining experience. A maître d's main job is to manage the front of the house (dining area) to ensure that the turnover of tables is smooth, that the atmosphere is pleasant, and that guests have a wonderful overall dining experience.

The following are just some of the duties for which a maître d' is responsible:

- Accepting reservations
- Ensuring that guests are seated quickly and properly
- Ensuring that dishes arrive promptly
- Inquiring about customers' satisfaction
- Supervising staff training and appearance
- Serving as a liaison between kitchen staff and food servers
- Troubleshooting problems
- Supervising restaurant cleanup and closing

Other responsibilities include ordering supplies, administering the staff payroll, and booking and budgeting events.

Working Conditions

The working conditions for the maître d' are pretty much the same as other positions throughout the restaurant, although the maître d' is less likely to have to lift and carry heavy objects. Maître d's communicate with customers and staff working in both the front and back of the restaurant, so they may be subject to falls in the back of the house where floors made slippery by spills may create such hazards. The front of the house, however, is a fairly safe working environment.

This is a stressful job due in large part to the high level of responsibility afforded to this position. The maître d' must be able to handle numerous tasks at once and make decisions quickly. In addition to stress resulting from such pressure, the hours are long and the maître d' is typically on his or her feet for most of the time. This makes for quite an exhausting day.

Training, Other Qualifications, and Advancement

Maître d's must have excellent communication and problem solving skills. They must enjoy working with people and be good at smoothing ruffled feathers. Resourcefulness and a practically endless amount of patience and tact are other attributes that will contribute to success in this field.

Maître d's must have a thorough knowledge of food, beverages, dining etiquette, and dining utensils. They must enjoy contributing to creating a memorable dining experience for others. The ability to work well under pressure is important. Last but not least, they must also be physically fit, as this is a very demanding job.

There are no specific educational requirements for maître d's. However, college courses in hotel and restaurant management or business administration are a definite asset if you want to pursue this profession. Many people start out working as a food server and work their way up to a maître d' position, as most skills can be learned on the job. Indeed, many employers will ask that maître d's have at least three years' experience as a head waiter or previous experience as a maître d'. Other useful experience for aspiring candidates includes any kind of work in a restaurant, hotel, airline, travel, or hospitality-related industry. (See The Maître d' Association website at www.maitre-d.com for more information.)

Earnings

Depending upon the establishment, you may be paid a salary or by the hour. Starting salaries average a low of about $25,000 to a high of $34,000, depending on the type of establishment and whether it is located in an urban setting.

Employment Outlook

The employment outlook for maître d's roughly corresponds to the health of the tourism and hospitality industries and the overall economy, since restaurants, hotels, cruise ships, and other places of employment for maître d's thrive when these are stable. In good economic times, people have more disposable income to spend on dining out, keeping restaurants in business and maître d's employed. According to the National Restaurant Association, as of April 2005, the outlook for the industry is positive with most restaurant owners reporting good sales and an optimistic outlook for the future. This should bode well for the security of maître d' positions in the near future.

Sommeliers

A sommelier is a wine expert employed by fine dining restaurants, wineries, or large beer, wine, and spirit stores to help people choose wines to pair with foods or purchase for gifts. Because restaurants employ most sommeliers, this section will focus on the duties of sommeliers in such a setting.

Sommeliers are experts in all aspects of fine drinking. They must be able to speak with authority about the wine areas of the world and their products; know the principal grape varieties used in winemaking; and present and serve wines, brandies, spirits, and liqueurs. They may also be required to have some expertise in beers and ciders, including the process of making them and the reasons for the variations in style between different products.

Additional duties of sommeliers include creating a wine list, managing the cellar, and keeping the cellar stocked. They may have to select, prepare, and position glassware necessary for the service of drinks in the lounge, restaurant, function room, or private suite. And they must be able to address questions and concerns in a diplomatic manner.

Working Conditions

Sommeliers have slightly better working conditions than maître d's. Sommeliers typically experience less stress because they do not have to supervise and coordinate the various positions. They rarely spend time in the back of the house or kitchen; instead, they spend most of their time in the wine storage area or cellar and in the front of the house helping patrons select wines to pair with their meals. Working conditions are generally safe and pleasant for most sommeliers.

Training, Other Qualifications, and Advancement

There are many educational programs for those considering a career as a sommelier. The Court of Master Sommeliers (www.courtof ms.com) is one such educational program. Started in the United Kingdom, this well-respected program landed in the United States in 1977. It offers training in three levels; graduates attain the designation of Master Sommelier.

Other educational opportunities can be found through the Culinary Institute of America's Professional Wine Certification Programs (www.prochef.com). Introductory courses for most programs include topics such as production methods of wines and spirits; pairing food and wine; and beginning wine tasting skills and describing wine characteristics. More advanced courses include service and salesmanship and honing wine tasting skills.

Most sommeliers spend some time under the tutelage of a seasoned sommelier. There is no set amount of time for this kind of apprenticeship, but it usually lasts for a least a year. During this learning period, the new sommelier will not only refine his or her taste for wine and spirits, but he or she will also learn how to select and stock a creative wine list.

Visit the following websites for information about wine and sommeliers: International Sommelier Guild (www.international sommelier.com), Sommelier Jobs (www.sommelierjobs.com), Wine Institute (www.wineinstitute.org), Wine Spectator Online (www .winespectator.com), and Wine Tasting (www.winetasting.org).

Earnings

Salary is often commensurate with experience, education, and training. According to the *Princeton Review* (www.princetonreview .com), the average starting salary for sommeliers is $20,000, after five years it's $30,000, and after ten to fifteen years it's $40,000. Of course, pay will be higher in the more upscale restaurants and in larger cities. In some places of employment, a bonus program linked to wine and beverage profits also may be available. Health and insurance benefits are often additional benefits of the job. Because sommeliers with a good reputation and solid experience are so much in demand, some employers may even pay relocation costs.

Employment Outlook

Because sommeliers are generally found only in upscale restaurants, hotels, and resorts, there are not many positions available even in the best of times. In good economic times when the restaurant industry is flourishing, more jobs will be available. Sommeliers generally report a high level of personal satisfaction in their jobs, making turnover fairly low. Your best bet for improving your chance of getting a good job as a sommelier is to acquire the best education and training in the area and be aggressive at networking and marketing yourself. Once you build a reputation, which may take up to fifteen years, greater opportunities will be available to you.

Meat Cutters

Meat cutters—also commonly known as butchers—must be expertly skilled in cutting down beef, veal, lamb, and pork from full, half, or quarter carcasses to serving portions that are cut, trimmed, and prepared to the chef's orders. In grocery stores, wholesale establishments that supply meat to restaurants, and institutional food service facilities, butchers and meat cutters separate wholesale cuts of meat into retail cuts or individually sized servings. They cut meat into steaks and chops, shape and tie roasts, and grind beef for sale as chopped meat. Boneless cuts are prepared with the use of knives, slicers, or power cutters, while band saws are required to carve bone-in pieces. Butchers and meat cutters in retail food stores also may weigh, wrap, and label the cuts of meat; arrange them in refrigerated cases for display; and prepare special cuts to fill unique orders.

Working Conditions

In 2002 approximately 132,000 people worked as meat cutters or butchers. Most were employed in retail food stores. The rest worked in wholesale stores, restaurants, hotels, hospitals, and other institutions. Jobs for meat cutters are located in almost every city and town in the nation.

Meat cutters, like the lesser-trained meat trimmers presented in the previous chapter, work in cold rooms designed to prevent meat from spoiling. The low temperatures and the need to stand for long periods and to lift heavy pieces of meat demand physical strength and stamina. Meat cutters must be careful when working with sharp tools, especially those that are powered. In addition, health and safety standards require clean and sanitary work areas to prevent meat from spoiling.

Training, Other Qualifications, and Advancement

Most meat cutters acquire their skills on-the-job. Although some are informally trained, most learn through apprenticeship programs. A few meat cutters learn their skills by attending private schools specializing in this trade. However, graduates of these schools often need additional training and experience to work as meat cutters. The training period for highly skilled butchers at the retail level may be one or two years.

Generally, on-the-job trainees begin by doing odd jobs, such as removing bones and fat from manufacturing cuts. Under the guidance of skilled meat cutters, they learn about the proper use of tools and equipment and how to prepare various cuts. After demonstrating skill with tools, they learn to divide quarters into primal cuts and to divide primal cuts into retail and individual portions. Trainees may learn how to cut and prepare fish and poultry, roll and tie roasts, prepare sausage, and cure meat. Later, they may learn marketing operations such as inventory control, meat buying, and recordkeeping. In addition, growing concern about the safety of meats has led employers to offer numerous safety seminars and extensive training in food safety to employees.

Meat cutters who learn the trade through apprenticeship programs generally complete two years of supervised on-the-job training that may be supplemented by classroom work. When the training period ends, apprentices are given a meat-cutting test, which is observed by their employer. In union shops, a union member also is present during the exam. Apprentices who pass the test qualify as meat cutters. Those who fail the exam may repeat it at a later time. In some areas, apprentices may become meat cutters without completing the entire training program, if they can pass the meat-cutting test.

Most employers prefer applicants who have a high school diploma and the potential to develop into meat department managers. Other skills important in meat cutting are manual dexterity, good depth perception, color discrimination, and good eye-hand coordination. A pleasant personality, a neat appearance, and the ability to communicate clearly are important qualifications when meat cutters wait on customers. Better-than-average strength is needed to lift heavy pieces of meat.

In terms of advancement, meat cutters may progress to supervisory jobs, such as meat department managers in supermarkets. A few become meat buyers for wholesalers and supermarket chains.

Some cutters even become grocery store managers or open their own meat markets.

Earnings

Earnings vary by industry, skill, geographic region, and educational level. The median annual earnings of butchers and meat cutters in 2002 were $25,500. The middle 50 percent earned between $19,440 and $34,140, the lowest 10 percent earned less than $15,490, and the highest 10 percent earned more than $42,330. Butchers and meat cutters employed at the retail level typically earn more than those in manufacturing. Median annual earnings in the industries employing the largest numbers of butchers and meat cutters in 2002 were as follows:

Other general merchandise stores	$30,670
Grocery stores	$27,230
Specialty food stores	$22,280
Animal slaughtering and processing	$20,630

Many meat cutters are members of the United Food and Commercial Workers International Union (www.ufcw.org).

Employment Outlook

As the nation's population continues to grow, the demand for meat, poultry, and seafood should continue to increase. Successful marketing by the poultry industry is likely to increase demand for chicken and ready-to-heat products. Similarly, the increasing availability of prepared meat cuts that are lower in fat and more nutritious promises to stimulate the consumption of red meat.

Unfortunately, employment of butchers and meat cutters who work primarily in retail stores is expected to continue to decline as it has for the past several years. This is because automation and the consolidation of the animal slaughtering and processing industries are enabling employers to transfer employment from higher-paid butchers to lower-wage slaughterers and meatpackers in meatpacking plants. At present, most red meat arrives at grocery stores partially cut up, but a growing share of meat is being delivered prepackaged, with additional fat removed, to wholesalers and retailers. This trend is resulting in less work and, thus, fewer jobs for retail butchers. That said, there continues to be a need for highly skilled and qualified individuals to fill the available positions.

5

UPPER-LEVEL POSITIONS

EXPERIENCE AND EDUCATION are two attributes that usually are required for higher-level management positions in the food service industry. As you read this chapter, you'll notice that most of these jobs require significantly more experience and education than those of previous chapters. In return, they boast greater levels of prestige, responsibility, and monetary compensation.

General Food Service Management Positions

Management positions in the food service industry are very diverse. In addition to restaurant operations, there are management positions available in marketing, publishing, the military, and food service production. Management positions exist in large and small corporations and offices, schools and universities, privately owned restaurants, sporting complexes, hotels, museums, factories, and performing arts centers. In short, wherever there's an entry-level food service worker, there will also be an upper-level worker to manage him or her.

There is no typical workday in the industry, thanks to the many types of food service outlets. In short, however, managers interview, hire, train, and, when necessary, fire employees. Retaining good employees is a major challenge facing food service managers. Managers recruit employees at career fairs, contact schools that offer academic programs in hospitality or culinary arts, and arrange for newspaper advertising to attract applicants. Managers oversee the training of new employees and explain the establishment's policies and practices. They schedule work hours, making sure that enough workers are present to cover each shift. Furthermore, on a daily basis, food service managers may determine what staff and equipment are needed for dining halls, kitchens, and meat-cutting plants; estimate food budgets; set standards for food storage and preparation; and maintain nutritional and sanitary standards at food service facilities.

Working Conditions

A typical workday is a long one for most food service managers. Many individuals work anywhere from ten to fifteen hours per day, up to six days a week, especially those in the restaurant sector. Managers of institutional food service facilities, such as school, factory, or office cafeterias, work more regular hours because the operating hours of these establishments usually conform to that of the business or facility they serve. However, hours for many managers are unpredictable.

Training, Other Qualifications, and Advancement

Managers must possess a range of qualities to be good at their jobs. They must be good communicators. They need to speak well, often in several languages, with a diverse clientele and staff. They must motivate employees to work as a team, to ensure that food and service meet appropriate standards. Managers also must be clear and concise in their communications to ensure that orders are unambiguous in a fast-paced environment. And they must be fair to handle conflicts amongst staff to everyone's satisfaction.

Experience in the field and education are essential. Many experienced food and beverage preparation and service workers are promoted into managerial positions; however, applicants with a master's or bachelor's degree in restaurant and institutional food service management should have the best job opportunities. In general, a four-year college degree is required to obtain a management position. Course content typically includes the following:

- Food service operations and management
- Resource management
- Nutritional meal planning
- Hotel management

Advancement involves moving from assistant manager to manager and then managing increasingly larger and more profitable departments and businesses. Perhaps the ultimate promotion is to that of owner. More than 35 percent of restaurant managers are self-employed or own the place they run. (Additional information on running your own business is presented in Chapter 7.)

Earnings

In 2002 the median annual earnings of salaried food service managers were $35,790. The middle 50 percent earned between $27,910 and $47,120, the lowest 10 percent earned less than

$21,760, and the highest 10 percent earned more than $67,490. Median annual earnings in the industries employing the largest numbers of food service managers were as follows:

Special food services	$40,720
Traveler accommodations	$39,210
Nursing care facilities	$33,910
Limited-service eating places	$33,590
Elementary and secondary schools	$31,210

Keep in mind that these figures are national averages and that salaries for individual positions could be considerably higher; it is not unusual for some food service directors to make $60,000 to $70,000 a year. Furthermore, many management positions will also include benefits, such as bonus sales programs, stock in the company, and complimentary meals for the individual and his or her family.

Employment Outlook

The employment outlook for food service managers is positive. According to the U.S. Department of Labor, manager jobs in special food services, an industry that includes food service contractors and excludes the restaurant industry, will increase as hotels, schools, health care facilities, and other businesses contract out their food services to firms in this industry. This affects management positions in other areas. While food service manager jobs are still expected to increase in hotels, schools, and health care facilities, growth will be slowed as contracting out becomes even more common.

Wealth of Management Opportunities

There are so many different management possibilities in the vast field of food service that it would be impossible to cover them all in detail in one small book. Therefore, the following descriptions are just snapshots of a range of different management and supervisory titles and their responsibilities. Experience in the field and continuing formal education will help you identify the areas that interest you.

Restaurant Manager

Managers are responsible for efficiency, quality, and courtesy in all phases of a food service operation. In large organizations, the managers may direct supervisory personnel at the next lower level. In smaller operations, they might supervise kitchen and dining room staffs directly. A thorough knowledge of the responsibilities of all restaurant staff is necessary. A more detailed description of this popular position follows later in this chapter.

Assistant Manager

Assistant managers perform specialized supervisory duties under the manager's direction. They must be capable of filling in when the manager is absent and thus must have good management skills and familiarity with overall food service operations.

Food Production Manager

This position entails responsibility for all food preparation and supervision of kitchen staff. Workers must possess leadership skills and have knowledge of food preparation techniques, quality and sanitation standards, and cost-control methods.

Personnel Director

Personnel directors usually are employed in larger restaurants, food service chains, or as specialists in hotel or institutional food service operations. Personnel directors are responsible for hiring and training food service personnel and for administering employee relations, benefits, safety, and communications programs.

Menu Planner

Menu planners select all food items offered on menus. They must know food service costs, preparation techniques and equipment, and consumer trends and preferences. This position usually requires a college or associate degree in dietetics or foods and nutrition. Restaurant managers, food production managers, or chefs may have these responsibilities assigned to them.

Merchandising Supervisor

Merchandising supervisors plan and carry out advertising and promotional programs to increase sales. Creativity and the ability to work with printers, artists, writers, and other suppliers are necessary. In addition, they must know their employer's food service operation thoroughly, be able to apply market research techniques, and be skilled in budgeting and planning. This position usually requires a college degree in advertising, marketing, merchandising, or a related field.

Purchasing Agent or Storeroom Supervisor

The purchasing agent or storeroom supervisor orders, receives, inspects, and stores all goods shipped by suppliers and oversees distribution to different food preparation departments. Requirements include inventory management skill, knowledge of good food storage practices, and up-to-date knowledge of market prices. Sometimes these duties are assigned to the manager or chef.

Director of Recipe Development

This director creates new recipes for the menus of larger restaurants, restaurant chains, institutions, and food production companies. Thorough knowledge of food preparation and the ability to apply this knowledge creatively are required.

Military Food Service Manager

The military services employ about five hundred food service managers. They are responsible for cooking and serving food at mess halls, directing the operation of dining halls, and supervising officers. After job training, food service managers either may work independently or under the supervision of other officers. With experience, they may manage one or more large facilities.

Restaurant Managers

The success of food service operations depends largely on the skills, abilities, and imagination of their management. Restaurant management can be demanding, varied, fast-paced, and highly rewarding. A modern restaurant is a complex operation, with the restaurant manager at its hub. Restaurant managers must be able to work efficiently behind the scenes, coordinating a wide variety of staff and administrative functions. They must be able to work effectively with the public as spokespeople, promoters, and goodwill ambassadors.

Restaurant managers have many important responsibilities. They are responsible for hiring, training, and directing restaurant staff members; determining work schedules; and setting personnel policies. In addition, they may be responsible for administering employee benefit programs. Keeping abreast of costs and maintaining accurate inventories are essential because managers are responsible for the purchase of all supplies and equipment.

Supervising advertising programs and working with the food production staff to create menus with customer appeal are also part of the restaurant manager's duties. The manager must stay in touch with changing needs and wants in the marketplace, help establish the "personality" of the restaurant, and be adept in dealing with the public, listening to suggestions, and handling complaints with diplomacy. In a large restaurant, many of these duties would be taken care of by the assistant manager, food production manager, personnel director, menu planner, merchandising supervisor, or director of recipe development. In general, the smaller the operation, the more diversified the duties of a restaurant manager.

Working Conditions

Food service managers are among the first to arrive in the morning and the last to leave at night. Long hours—from twelve to fifteen per day, fifty or more per week, and sometimes seven days a week—are common in the restaurant business. Night and weekend work are very common.

Restaurant managers sometimes experience the pressures of coordinating a wide range of functions. Managers should be calm, flexible, and able to work through emergencies, such as a fire or flood, to ensure everyone's safety. Managers also should be able to fill in for absent workers on short notice. When problems occur, it is the manager's responsibility to resolve them with minimal disruption to customers. The job can be hectic, and dealing with irate customers or uncooperative employees can be stressful.

Managers also may experience the typical minor injuries of other restaurant workers, such as muscle aches, cuts, or burns. They might endure physical discomfort from moving tables or chairs to accommodate large parties, receiving and storing daily supplies from vendors, or making minor repairs to furniture or equipment. However, the working environment is usually clean, well lit, and air-conditioned.

Training, Other Qualifications, and Advancement

A good manager possesses a combination of business acumen, people skills, drive, and fairness. To be successful, a restaurant manager must have good business skills and know how to set prices to make a profit. He or she must take responsibility for the restaurant's accounts and records and must know and comply with all food service laws and regulations, especially those concerned with licensing, health, and sanitation. A manager must know every aspect of the restaurant business thoroughly, because it is the manager who is called on to act as troubleshooter for all restaurant operations. Additionally, managers should have initiative, self-discipline, and the ability to organize and direct the work of others. They must be able to solve problems and concentrate on details.

While experience generally is the most important consideration in selecting managers, employers are increasingly emphasizing college education. Completion of at least a two-year associate degree program at a community college or a bachelor's degree program in hotel and restaurant management at a four-year college or university, will enable applicants to enter restaurant management at a higher level. Because more aspiring managers are seeking formal training, applicants to these programs may face increasing competition in the coming years. Sometimes, large restaurant chains sponsor specialized, on-the-job management-training programs that enable trainees to rotate among various departments and receive a thorough knowledge of the restaurant's operation.

Many community colleges, technical institutes, and the American Hotel and Lodging Educational Institute (www.ei-ahla.org) offer management courses. (See Chapter 8 for additional information about education and training.) Included in many college programs in hotel and restaurant management are courses in hotel administration, accounting and finance, economics, housekeeping, food service management, catering, and hotel maintenance engineering. Part-time or summer work in hotels and restaurants is encouraged. The experience gained and the contact with employers may benefit students when they seek a job after graduation.

Earnings

According to the U.S. Department of Labor, in 2002, managers in full-service restaurants received a median salary of $37,280. Managers of fast-food restaurants earn considerably less while managers of the largest restaurants and institutional food service facilities often had annual salaries in excess of $50,000. In addition to a salary, most managers received an annual bonus or incentive payment based on their performance. Bonus payments may range from $2,000 to $10,000 a year. Finally, most salaried restaurant and food service managers received free meals, sick leave, health and life insurance, and one to three weeks of paid vacation a year, depending on length of service.

Employment Outlook

In 2002, food service managers held approximately 386,000 jobs. Employment of restaurant managers is expected to grow faster than the average for all occupations through the year 2006, as additional restaurants are built and chain and franchise operations spread. Seasonal employment opportunities will be available in resort establishments that are open only part of the year.

Applicants with college degrees in hotel and restaurant administration will have an advantage in seeking entry-level positions and, later, advancement. Those working at restaurant chains may have better opportunities for advancement than those employed by independently owned establishments, because employees can transfer to another hotel or motel in the chain or to the central office if an opening occurs.

Dietitians and Nutritionists

Dietitians and nutritionists plan food and nutrition programs and supervise the preparation and serving of meals. They help to prevent and treat illnesses by promoting healthy eating habits and recommending dietary modifications, such as the use of less salt for those with high blood pressure or the reduction of fat and sugar intake for those who are overweight. These workers are most interested in how food influences body function.

Dietitians and nutritionists work in a variety of settings. They manage food service systems for institutions such as hospitals and schools, promote sound eating habits through education, and conduct research. Dietitians provide nutritional counseling to individuals and groups. They set up and supervise food service systems for institutions such as hospitals and schools. They promote sound eating habits through education and research. Increased public interest in nutrition has led to job opportunities in food manufacturing, advertising, and marketing. In these areas, dietitians analyze foods, prepare literature for distribution, or report on issues such as the nutritional content of recipes, dietary fiber, or vitamin supplements. Among dietitians, major areas of specialization include clinical, community, management, administration, and consultant dietetics.

Clinical dietitians provide nutritional services for patients in institutions such as hospitals and nursing care facilities. They assess patients' nutritional needs, develop and implement nutrition programs, and evaluate and report the results. They also confer with doctors and other health care professionals to coordinate medical and nutritional needs. Some clinical dietitians specialize in the management of overweight patients or the care of critically ill or renal (kidney) and diabetic patients. In addition, clinical dietitians in nursing care facilities, small hospitals, or correctional facilities may manage the food service department.

Community dietitians counsel individuals and groups on nutritional practices designed to prevent disease and promote health. Working in places such as public health clinics, home health agencies, and health maintenance organizations, community dietitians evaluate individual needs, develop nutritional care plans, and instruct individuals and their families. Dietitians working in home health agencies provide instruction on grocery shopping and food preparation to the elderly and to individuals who have special needs and/or children.

Management dietitians oversee large-scale meal planning and preparation in health care facilities, company cafeterias, prisons, and schools. They hire, train, and direct other dietitians and food service workers; budget for and purchase food, equipment, and supplies; enforce sanitary and safety regulations; and prepare records and reports.

Consultant dietitians work under contract with health care facilities or in their own private practices. They perform nutrition screenings for their clients and offer advice on diet-related concerns such as weight loss or cholesterol reduction. Some work for wellness programs, sports teams, supermarkets, and other nutrition-related businesses. They may consult with food service managers, providing expertise in sanitation, safety procedures, menu development, budgeting, and planning.

Administrative dietitians are the ones the food service industry is interested in. They apply the principles of nutrition and sound management to large-scale meal planning and preparation, such as that done in hospitals, prisons, company cafeterias, schools, and other institutions. They supervise the planning, preparation, and service of meals. They select, train, and direct food service supervisors and workers. They also budget for and purchase food, equipment, and supplies; enforce sanitary and safety regulations; and prepare records and reports.

Working Conditions

In 2002, dietitians and nutritionists held about forty-nine thousand jobs. More than half of all jobs were in hospitals, nursing care facilities, outpatient care centers, or offices of physicians and other health practitioners. State and local government agencies provided about one job in five—mostly in correctional facilities, health departments, and other public health-related areas.

Some dietitians and nutritionists were employed in special food services, an industry that includes firms that provide food services on contract to facilities such as colleges and universities, airlines, correctional institutions, and company cafeterias. Other jobs were in public and private educational services, community care facilities for the elderly (which includes assisted-living facilities), individual and family services, and home health care services. Some dietitians were self-employed, working as consultants to institutions such as hospitals and nursing care facilities or providing dietary counseling to individual clients.

Most full-time dietitians and nutritionists work a regular forty-hour week, although some, especially those in commercial food service, work weekends. About 25 percent of registered dietitians work part-time. Overall, the places in which dietitians and nutritionists usually work are clean, well-lit, and well-ventilated areas. However, some dietitians work in warm, congested kitchens. Many dietitians and nutritionists are on their feet for much of the workday.

Training, Other Qualifications, and Advancement

The basic educational requirement for dietitians is a bachelor's degree, with a major in foods and nutrition or institutional management. Some of the required college courses include food and nutrition, institutional management, chemistry, microbiology, physiology, sociology, and economics. It also is possible to prepare for this profession by receiving an advanced degree in nutrition, food service management, or related sciences and providing evidence of qualifying work experience. High school students interested in becoming a dietitian or nutritionist should take courses in biology, chemistry, mathematics, health, and communications.

According to the U.S. Department of Labor, of the forty-six states and jurisdictions with laws governing dietetics, thirty require licensure, fifteen require certification, and one requires registration. The Commission on Dietetic Registration of the American Dietetic Association (www.cdrnet.org) awards the registered dietitian credential to those who pass a certification exam after completing their academic course work and supervised experience. Because practice requirements vary by state, you should investigate the requirements of your state before sitting for any exam.

As of 2003, there were about 230 bachelor's and master's degree programs approved by the ADA's Commission on Accreditation for Dietetics Education (CADE). Supervised practice experience can be acquired in two ways: The first requires the completion of a CADE-accredited coordinated program. As of 2003, there were more than fifty accredited programs, which combined academic and supervised practice experience and generally lasted four to five years. The second option requires the completion of nine hundred hours of supervised practice experience in any of the 264 CADE-accredited/approved internships. These internships may be full-time programs lasting six to twelve months or part-time programs lasting two years. Students interested in research, advanced clinical positions, or public health may need an advanced degree.

Areas of specialty and opportunities for advancement are abundant in this field. Experienced dietitians may advance to assistant director, associate director, or director of a dietetic department or may become self-employed. Some dietitians specialize in areas such as renal or pediatric dietetics. Others may leave the occupation to become sales representatives for equipment, pharmaceutical, or food manufacturers.

Earnings

In 2002, median annual earnings of dietitians and nutritionists were $41,170. The middle 50 percent earned between $33,210 and $49,830, the lowest 10 percent earned less than $25,520, and the highest 10 percent earned more than $58,700. Median annual earnings in general medical and surgical hospitals, which employed the largest number of dietitians and nutritionists, were $41,910. According to the American Dietetic Association, median annual income for registered dietitians varied by practice area as follows:

Consultation and business	$60,000
Food and nutrition management	$55,000
Education and research	$54,800
Clinical nutrition/ambulatory care	$44,000
Clinical nutrition/long-term care	$43,300
Community nutrition	$43,200
Clinical nutrition/acute care	$40,800

Salaries also vary by years in practice, educational level, geographic region, and size of the community.

Employment Outlook

Employment of dietitians is expected to grow about as fast as the average for all occupations through 2012 as a result of increasing emphasis on disease prevention through improved dietary habits. A growing and aging population will boost the demand for meals and nutritional counseling in hospitals, nursing care facilities, schools, prisons, community health programs, and home health care agencies. Public interest in nutrition and increased emphasis on health education and prudent lifestyles will also spur demand, especially in management.

In addition to employment growth, job openings will result from the need to replace experienced workers who leave the occupation. On the one hand, employment growth for dietitians and nutritionists may be constrained if some employers substitute other workers, such as health educators, food service managers, and dietetic technicians. Growth also may be curbed by limitations on insurance reimbursement for dietetic services, but the overall outlook is a positive one.

6

ADDITIONAL FOOD SERVICE JOBS

ASIDE FROM THE obvious career positions in the food service industry, such as bartender, food server, and restaurant manager, there are numerous other positions available for people possessing a variety of skills and interests. This vast industry employs people who work outside the kitchens and offices of restaurants or other food serving establishments. Additional food service jobs include those working in the manufacturing and communications fields, consultants, lawyers, accountants, public relations specialists, marketing managers, purchasing agents, quality assurance officers, and administrative assistants. Many of these positions can be found in both the nonprofit and business sectors and in businesses both large and small.

While it is beyond the scope of this book to provide much detail on each of these positions, after reading this chapter, you should have a general idea of what the work entails. For additional information, you should conduct an online search using pertinent keywords, and check out the websites of associations, organizations, and journals listed in the appendixes. Consider this chapter to be window-shopping for your future career!

Manufacturing Workers

Workers in the food manufacturing sector of the food service industry link farmers and other agricultural producers with consumers. They do this by processing raw fruits, vegetables, grains, meats, and dairy products into finished goods ready for the grocer or wholesaler to sell to households, restaurants, or institutional food services. Food manufacturing workers perform tasks as varied as the many foods we eat.

The food manufacturing industry employs many different types of workers. More than half are production workers in plants or factories. These include skilled precision workers and less-skilled machine operators and laborers. Many other workers are needed to keep food manufacturing plants and equipment in good working order. Still other workers directly oversee the quality of both the work and the final products. Food may spoil if not properly packaged and promptly delivered, so packaging and transportation employees play a vital role in the industry.

The food manufacturing industry also employs a variety of managerial and professional workers. Managers include top executives, who make policy decisions; industrial production managers, who organize, direct, and control the operation of the manufacturing plant; and advertising, marketing, promotions, public relations, and sales managers, who direct advertising, sales promotion, and community relations programs. Finally, many sales workers, including sales representatives, wholesale and manufacturing, are needed to sell the manufactured goods to wholesale and retail establishments. Bookkeeping, accounting, and auditing clerks, as well as procurement clerks, keep track of the food products going into and out of the plant. Janitors and cleaners keep buildings clean and orderly.

Engineers, scientists, and technicians are becoming increasingly important as the food manufacturing industry implements new automation. These workers include industrial engineers, who plan equipment layout and workflow in manufacturing plants, emphasizing efficiency and safety. Also, mechanical engineers plan, design, and oversee the installation of tools, equipment, and machines. Chemists perform tests to develop new products and maintain the quality of existing products. Computer programmers and systems analysts develop the computer systems and programs that support management and scientific research. Food scientists and technologists work in research laboratories or on production lines to develop new products, test current ones, and control food quality.

Communications Workers

Those working in food service communications include writers, editors, and photographers. They disseminate information of interest to all those working in the various sectors of the food service industry—from restaurants to manufacturing. These workers provide the industry with information on food service products, promotions and trends, regional food service activities, and industry workshops and initiatives. These workers are in charge of posting content on company websites, as well as producing trade journals and magazines.

Food Service Consultants

Food service consultants are typically their own bosses, taking clients on a work-for-hire basis. These workers are specialists in many aspects of the food service industry—from marketing and advertising to menu and concept development. Food service consultants create hot concepts, products, menus, programs, and operations; plan customer-oriented, market-driven strategies to increase a business's sales, profits, and customer satisfaction; advise on building and renovation plans; and identify ways to reduce costs, increase efficiency, and improve quality. Individuals can make a good living as a food service consultant, but to do so they must have plenty of direct industry experience and be adept at building a clientele.

Lawyers

Laws govern every aspect of our society, and this includes the food service industry. Lawyers specializing in food service operations or the industry in general should always be consulted before purchasing, opening, and selling a food service business and in any contractual issues. As the food industry grows, the work of lawyers or attorneys takes on broader significance—they are employed to interpret the laws, rulings, and regulations pertaining to the food service industry.

Accountants

Owners and managers must have up-to-date financial information at their fingertips to help them make many different kinds of important decisions. Accountants and auditors prepare and analyze financial reports that furnish this kind of information. Accountants may be employed on a regular, semiregular, or per-service basis. Accountants employed full-time by large restaurant chains or other

food and facilities management services, such as Sodexho (www
.sodexhousa.com) may travel extensively to audit or work for clients
or branches of the organization.

Public Relations Specialists

Public relations workers help food service businesses build and
maintain a positive public reputation, which is crucial to the success of any food service operation, including hunger relief organizations. Public relations workers put together information that keeps
the public aware of their organization's policies, activities, and
accomplishments, and keeps management aware of public attitudes.
After preparing the information, they contact people in the media
who might be interested in printing, televising, or broadcasting
their materials. Preparing and delivering speeches, attending meet-
ings and community activities, and traveling out of town will all be
part of the job assigned to the public relations worker.

Marketing Managers

Marketing managers are responsible for compiling information on
the age, sex, and income level of a restaurant's potential clientele,
as well as dining habits and preferences. On this information, they
base their decisions of whether a restaurant would do well in a certain area. Marketing managers consider customer preferences and
suggest appropriate sales advertising techniques, including the tone
and content of print, radio, and television ads. These jobs are most
likely to be found in large food manufacturing and supply organizations rather than smaller businesses.

Purchasing Agents

Purchasing agents are responsible for obtaining goods and services of the quality required at the lowest possible cost. Also, it is their job to see that adequate materials and supplies are always available. Purchasing agents choose suppliers by comparing listings in catalogs, directories, and trade journals. They must meet with salespeople to discuss items to be purchased, examine samples, and attend demonstrations of equipment. Purchasing agents must be able to analyze the technical data in suppliers' proposals to make buying decisions and spend large amounts of money responsibly. The job requires the ability to work well both independently and with people. Purchasing agents need a good memory for details. Again, this type of job is typically found in a larger organization.

Quality Assurance Officers

In the food service industry, a quality assurance officer has a very important job. The cleanliness and sanitation practices of a food service operation are crucial elements to its success. The quality assurance officers are responsible for developing and implementing sanitation practices that will keep the restaurant in business. Responsibilities of a quality assurance officer may include some of the following:

- Monitor food packaging safety
- Conduct sanitation audits
- Inspect food quality with routine analyzing and testing of production batches and finished product
- Perform basic microbiological testing

- Assist in investigation, root cause, and corrective action for quality nonconformances
- Communicate with U.S. Department of Agriculture (www.usda.gov) inspectors

Food Brokers

Food brokers are also known as food vendors or, generally, salespeople. They sell everything from different foodstuffs to food-related products or services, but they tend to specialize in one area. Brokers are in charge of selling and stocking products to food sales outlets from supermarkets to convenience stores to corner grocers. People in this position need to have outgoing, friendly personalities and be willing to travel often for their job. Typically, a food broker will be responsible for selling to a particular region. These workers receive a base salary and usually also work on commission, meaning the more they sell, the more money they make.

Administrative Assistants

Administrative assistants play a very important role in large food service operations. They perform a variety of duties, including providing clerical and administrative support, assisting others with projects, and serving as the point person for the public.

Employers look for a variety of qualities in administrative assistants. In addition to a solid grounding in computer skills, the best candidates should have a good command of the English language, initiative, strong organizational abilities, and an aptitude for numbers. Because administrative assistants must be tactful in their dealings with many different people, discretion, judgment, and excellent communication skills are also important attributes.

Administrative positions are an excellent means of gaining entry to a company. If you have a strong desire to work for a particular company, but there aren't any positions open in your area, try landing an administrative assistant job. That way, you'll get your foot in the door and you can prove yourself to be an excellent candidate when the job finally does become available.

7

Running Your Own Business

Owning and operating a business is no easy task. Competition is keen in many segments of the food service industry, perhaps none more so than the restaurant sector. Almost every week, two hundred new restaurants open in the United States. But one year later, only forty will still be in business. A 20 percent success rate is not an encouraging figure, but this does not seem to discourage would-be restaurateurs. This is because business owners possess a creativity, drive, and vision that will be neither dissuaded nor discouraged by statistics.

No one can offer a guarantee for success, but there are steps to take to avoid common pitfalls and increase a venture's chance for success. While by no means inclusive, this chapter presents a few of the many things you'll need to consider if you hope to someday own and operate your own business, whether that be catering, running a restaurant, or opening a specialty foods store.

Developing a Plan

A plan of action is the most important step in starting up your business. A workable plan that outlines a concept in food service as well as a marketing research effort will be a critical aid to even the most experienced food service professionals. To create a comprehensive, well-thought-out plan, you'll need to calculate the precise initial investment requirements, apply for financing, determine what your operating expenses will be, and project break-even sales figures. The first step in doing this is to carefully consider all aspects of the business—from what will be served, who will be served, and product prices, to the size of staff and location of the establishment. To see if you're on the right path, start by answering the following questions:

- What kind of food will be served?
- What is the general price range?
- What type of service (fast-food, self-service, cafeteria, counter, table service) will be offered?
- What menu items will be offered?
- What kind of atmosphere is desired?
- Who are the anticipated clientele?
- What cooking methods will be used?
- What size staff is necessary?
- What kind of inventory is required?
- What hours will the restaurant operate?
- What are the projected sales?
- What amount of food should be prepared on-site?

In addition to answering these questions, you'll need to develop a plan for where your business is located, the need for the services you offer in the area you've chosen, and what kind of image you want to project.

Location is often key. For example, an event-catering business located in an upscale neighborhood next to several bridal salons will attract more of the targeted clientele than one located in a manufacturing district—that is, if you can afford the rent! This leads into the next step, which is developing a marketing study.

Developing a Marketing Study

Prospective restaurant owners often have a concept in mind, but they fail to do adequate marketing research to determine whether their ideas match the needs of the community. There are really very few original ideas, which means that conducting thorough and timely market research can help you identify whether there's a need for your services before you invest a lot of time and effort.

That's what marketing research is—a study of consumer needs and preferences. Marketing research also is an assessment of the local business environment. A market investigation will help the prospective business owner ascertain if a real demand exists for a particular kind of food service. It also will reveal if there is so much demand that an oversupply of similar establishments will mean fierce competition. Once you know who the potential customers are, what percentage of the population they represent, the competition you are up against, and the business traffic patterns by hours of the day, days of the week, and weekday versus weekend, you will be in a better position to supply the needs to your customers and to compete with other food service establishments in the locality.

You can compile most of this information yourself. The U.S. Census Bureau (www.census.gov) provides demographic profiles, income levels, and housing patterns for the nation as a whole and by segments—right down to city blocks. These data are available in printed form or can be accessed by computer, and you can even order an individualized computer printout. Furthermore, the U.S. government runs the Small Business Administration (SBA) site at www.sba.gov. This site offers a wide variety of useful information. Every state has at least one SBA district office, and there are multiple resource partners to support the needs of the small business community.

Professional organizations are another valuable source of information for conducting market research, as they usually have their finger on the pulse of industry trends. The National Restaurant Association has a tab on the website home page for industry research, or it can be found at www.restaurant.org/research. That is just one example of an industry source, but keep in mind that all aspects of food service—from food processing to advertising—will have similar organizations offering priceless information to the small business entrepreneur.

Most towns and cities of any size offer classes and seminars geared toward small business start-up concerns. Check out your local newspaper for ads and call a community college near you to inquire about classes. A small investment of time and money may save you considerably in the long run.

Doing a complete and thorough market survey takes time, but it's time well spent. The survey can keep you from opening a restaurant in a location where success is impossible, and it can greatly aid your case when you seek help in funding from financial institutions. These are just some suggestions for places to look for information. Your online bookstore or local library will have a variety of books on the topic to further assist you.

Choosing a Site

Once you have picked a suitable concept and verified the idea through market research, you must then research and settle upon a good location for the business. Any business's success probably depends most on a proper location. The location should position the restaurant where it can best attract and serve its anticipated clientele. As you consider locations, ask yourself the following questions:

- Is the space visible from the street?
- Are parking arrangements available?
- What types of businesses are currently in the area?
- Are there hidden costs involved in remodeling or construction?
- Is public transportation available and do taxicabs frequent the area?
- What are the peak traffic hours?
- Are there plans for growth in the area?
- What are the average sales of competitors in the area?
- How many households are in the area?

Many prospective restaurant owners believe that they can more easily enter the food service industry by buying a restaurant that is already in operation. Indeed, buying a building that doesn't need extensive remodeling can save considerable expense. For example, the high cost of complying with local building codes and constructing kitchen and dining space in a building that was used for something entirely different in its previous incarnation would be eliminated. Current building owners, who are running good operations but can't make their interest payment, may provide an excellent opportunity for a prospective owner. As little as 10 to 30 percent of the original construction costs may be all it takes to purchase a bankrupt business. The new owner probably will be able to realize good profits because there will be less debt to service.

Keep in mind, however, that a potential buyer should carefully investigate the reasons given for selling the business. The seller may offer poor health or retirement as the reason for selling, but through careful study of local conditions and market research, the prospective buyer might discover the real reason to be any number of issues, including declining business, lack of competitive strength, changes in the neighborhood, obsolete products or facilities, highway construction or rerouting, inability to collect accounts receivable, problems with creditors, or an expiring lease or franchise.

Scrutinizing your location site thoroughly will benefit you in the long run, and there are a variety of resources available to help you do just that. You can obtain useful information and data from the Department of Commerce (www.commerce.gov), the U.S. Small Business Administration (www.sba.gov), real estate agencies, a food service consultant, your accountant, your banker, and your insurance agent.

Codes, Ordinances, and Permits

Be sure to obtain information about local codes, ordinances, permits, and licenses as you research potential sites. A fire clearance, for example, depends on inspection. Some common codes include: fire, health, parking, occupancy, garbage, sewage, and loading zone. Both health and building codes usually require cost estimates and blueprints to be submitted before construction. If these are well prepared and planned, costly after-construction alterations will be minimized.

You will need to obtain several different kinds of licenses before opening a new restaurant. The purpose of a business license is taxation and regulation of the privilege of doing business in the city. Cities and towns often have various zoning regulations that control the location and the operation of all commercial activities, which means that you will need permission and licenses for operating certain kinds of businesses.

Specific licenses include a fictitious name license, or a DBA (Doing Business as . . .), which is a license that's needed if you plan to operate under a name other than your own. In addition, a business or sales tax license is required by some states. Finally, a liquor or beer and wine license is necessary if you plan to serve alcoholic beverages. These licenses usually require fingerprinting, an inspection, and often a period of time for local citizens to file any objections to the license. Some jurisdictions demand that you buy a license from a former owner rather than apply for a new one. Registration with the Internal Revenue Service (www.irs.gov) is compulsory for a liquor or beer and wine license.

Insurance

Every business that is open to the public requires the owner to have insurance. This includes product and personal liability as well as coverage on the space used for the business, equipment, any vehicles used for the business, and worker's compensation for any employees. The three main types of insurance you can purchase to protect your business are liability, property coverage, and business interruption (for example, shutdown due to a natural disaster). There are steps you can take to safeguard the health of your employees, such as keeping the workplace clean, well lit, and free of clutter, but there are many other circumstances you cannot control. Consider insurance a necessary expense that will protect you financially should an unforeseen accident occur.

Financial Record Keeping

Financial record keeping or accounting is not difficult, but it can be time-consuming, and business owners are incredibly busy people. In addition, you may be more interested in marketing your business and the execution of your services than in keeping the books. Regardless, to properly run your business, you'll need to keep track of income, expenses, and profit or loss, both to determine business growth and for tax purposes. This is something you can do yourself or you can hire an accountant to help you set up a record-keeping system that you can then maintain, thus saving you valuable time. Additional information on record keeping and business taxes is available from your local library, online and retail bookstores, the Internal Revenue Service (www.irs.gov), local Small Business Administration (www.sba.gov) office, or Small Business Development Center (www.asbdc-us.org).

Menu Planning

The menu performs a major function for every food service business. After all, the quality and desirability of your product will have a substantial effect on whether your business succeeds. The menu is more than just a collection of foods from which your customers will choose. In fact, the menu serves a variety of purposes, including:

- Defining your restaurant
- Reflecting your concept
- Setting the tone of your restaurant

- Attracting your customers
- Providing a guide for ordering, purchasing, and estimating income
- Determining the layout of the kitchen
- Determining what skills your staff will need
- Determining storage requirements
- Determining what special equipment is needed

The menu should never be static. You may have to make modifications to it as you get further along into the process of setting up your business and throughout conducting your marketing research. Potential clientele, seasonal availability of foods, community preferences, suitable combinations of dishes, and alternatives for leftovers will all have an influence on your menu. Those restaurateurs who can limit the menu and still do a high-volume business will reap the greatest profits, but restaurant image and appeal sometimes prohibit this. Price is also a very important factor when drawing up your menu. Overpricing has killed many new operations. A general rule of thumb often used in the food service industry is that a menu price should not be more than double or triple the wholesale food cost.

Records on how frequently menu items are served help owners reorder the correct quantity of food. Many restaurateurs say personal computer systems often pay for themselves by tracking menu items in this way.

Kitchen Plan and Equipment

The kitchen is vitally important to any food service operation, and careful planning should be given to stocking it as necessary and at an economical cost. Just a few of the commonly purchased items for many food service businesses include short-order griddles or grills, broilers, double-decker ovens, ranges, dryers, full-size refrigerators, walk-in freezers, and dishwashing machines.

Costs for new kitchen equipment can run into thousands of dollars. Equipment companies usually do not extend more than sixty to ninety days' credit to customers, so many of these purchases must come from start-up capital. Sometimes equipment leasing arrangements are also possible. The benefit of leasing arrangements is that they allow you to stretch payments over a longer period of time. The downside, however, is that they usually include substantial interest charges. Remember that cost is not the only consideration when choosing equipment. Other important factors that should be weighed include the manufacturer's reliability, repair service availability, and the quality of repair if the manufacturer provides it.

In addition to stocking the kitchen, a solid kitchen plan should take into consideration the following:

- Workspace needed for food preparation
- Adequate space to pass food from the cooks to the food servers
- Sufficient aisle space for food servers to deliver the food to the patrons
- Cleanup center for washing dishes and disposing of garbage
- Separate area for delivery of inventory

Getting a Good Financial Start

It takes a lot of money to open your own business. In fact, 85 percent of investment costs go toward start-up expenses. Start-up expenses include such items as wiring, plumbing, painting, labor, materials, kitchen fixtures and equipment, furniture, and two months' lease deposit.

Whether you decide on equity financing, which is money from investors, or debt financing, which is money from a financial establishment, obtaining it can be difficult. A typical bank loan requires furnishing a great deal of information, including a detailed report on the loan's purpose, personal financial statements, a list of partners or corporate officers, and projected financial statements for the first one or two years. In addition, most banks require you to find half the financing yourself. This can come from relatives, friends, business associates, or partners, but not from another loan. By demonstrating your viability with market studies and by having bookkeeping, accounting, and marketing systems in place, you may strengthen your position with a financial establishment. Most small business owners look to both equity and debt financing as sources for funding.

The federal government is another potential source of funding. Although the process for obtaining them is often difficult, the loans can be below market interest rates and with longer payback periods. The Small Business Administration (www.sba.gov) will guarantee up to 90 percent of a commercial loan. On rare occasions, the SBA may make a direct loan if the applicant can prove he or she cannot find funding elsewhere.

No matter where you go for financing, it is a good idea to have enough capital to cover at least two to six months of payroll and food costs. Be forewarned: one of the major causes of small business failures is insufficient financing. So, when drawing up your financial requirements, make sure to include money for these common start-up costs:

- Initial lease deposit or down payment on property
- Remodeling or making improvements
- Purchase of equipment and furnishings
- License payments
- Utility and insurance deposits
- Initial food inventory
- Initial advertising
- Consultant fees (lawyer, accountant, kitchen designer, menu designer, and so forth)
- Initial payroll and payroll taxes

Also, be sure to build a cushion for the unexpected, such as a delay in opening.

Staffing

Many times potential restaurant owners overestimate their capabilities. Although sometimes necessary, it is difficult for an owner to be a personnel manager, financier, chef, food purchaser, tax expert, and public relations expert all at the same time. Interviewing, hiring, and training people can be a time-consuming and nerve-racking process, but time invested in this process at the beginning will pay off substantially in the end.

Franchise Opportunities

Many first-time restaurateurs are attracted by the opportunities of a restaurant franchise. The 80 percent survival rate of establishments franchised by reputable chains has a lot to do with their appeal. Franchised businesses account for billions in annual sales and nearly a third of total U.S. retail sales, making them a strong business venture. That said, in recent years, it has become increasingly difficult to break into the franchise business, but it is not impossible.

What Is a Restaurant Franchise?

Franchising is a form of licensing by which the owner (the franchisor) obtains distribution through affiliated dealers (the franchisees). Franchise agreements call for the parent company to give an independent businessperson rights to a successful restaurant concept and trademark, plus assistance in organizing, training, merchandising, and managing. In return for these rights and assistance, the franchisee pays the company a franchise fee and monthly royalties.

Examine the Franchisor Carefully

The prospective restaurateur should examine the franchisor's claims and credentials as thoroughly as possible. Detailed investigation into the backgrounds and current business practices of operations is essential. Carefully examine franchise packages to see where the best deals on franchise fees and royalties are offered.

A disclosure statement, sometimes called an offering circular or prospectus, is available from every franchisor. This disclosure statement will prove an invaluable help in comparing one franchise with another, understanding the risks involved, and learning what to expect and what not to expect from the franchise you finally decide on.

A reputable franchise company should be able to provide you with the following:

- A site, usually a freestanding building that is leased to the franchisee
- Exclusive territorial rights
- Any exclusively developed equipment
- Licensed use of trademark, inventory system, exclusive recipes, and techniques
- Training courses and operations manuals
- Continuing operations assistance for a specified percentage of gross sales
- Inspections by company supervisors, who will evaluate the operation
- Consultation on reducing costs and improving efficiency and profits
- Equipment
- Suppliers
- Advertising

Prospective franchisees are carefully interviewed by company sales directors, who evaluate applicants' financial assets, character, and work history. Franchisors look for people who are eager to become independent operators, but who will conform to the company's guidelines. Applicants who meet these qualifications will then have to pay various fees. These include an initial franchise fee; continuing royalty fees, which can range from 2.5 to 8 percent of the unit gross sales; advertising contributions of about 2 to 4 percent of gross sales; food, labor, and paper costs; equipment purchase or rental costs; and rent.

The Value of an Attorney

Anyone considering entering into a franchise agreement should employ an attorney to determine if the contract's provisions protect his or her interests. Even the most intelligent and seasoned businessperson can be confused by legal lingo. Be certain the lawyer does a thorough job of checking out the following items:

- Length of contract
- Royalty charges
- Fixed charges
- Purchasing requirements
- Quotas
- Arbitration privileges
- How the contract can be terminated
- How the company can terminate the franchisee

Overall, franchising is an excellent way for a person without special skills to be trained in every aspect of the food service industry, but be certain that you have all the facts and information you need to make a wise decision. The cost of legal advice at the outset is invariably less than the cost of later representation to solve legal problems that could have been avoided in the beginning.

For more information, see the following websites: Franchise Equity Group (www.fegroup.com), Franchise Handbook: On-line A–Z (www.franchise1.com), and Minority Franchising (www.minorityfranchising.com).

Catering Opportunities

Every day there are thousands of celebratory events taking place, including weddings, bar and bat mitzvahs, birthdays, anniversaries, and other celebrations marking life events. Many of these events serve food prepared by a catering business. Catering is a $5 billion a year industry with a secure future. As long as couples get married and corporations host annual parties and conferences, caterers will be needed.

Starting your own catering business can be rewarding in a variety of ways, both financially and personally. Each event you cater will be a unique way to highlight your food and presentation skills. You will interact with people of all ages and personality types. With these rewards, however, comes demanding work, for which you will need physical stamina to endure long days and the ability to work well under the pressure of tight deadlines.

All About Location

You can operate your catering business out of your home if you have the proper equipment, or from a commercial space. If you choose to run your business from your home, be aware that the local health department has rules and regulations that you must adhere to in order to be in compliance with the law. For example, state laws often require food preparation areas to be set apart from the part of your home where you conduct business or activities of daily living. To ensure this, the health department may have to inspect your home. There must also be separate sinks for food, utensil washing, and cleaning to avoid contamination. Running your business from a commercial space means that you'll have all the start-up costs and need for licenses described above.

Catering Business Plan

You will also need to conduct market research and create a business plan for starting up your own catering business. Prior to starting a catering business, you will need to determine the types of foods and events you would like to cater. For example, do you want to do cakes, receptions, seated dinners, box lunches, picnics, hors d'oeuvres, or dessert only? Also, do you want to prepare everything from scratch or use prepared foods or a combination of both?

Part of creating a good business plan is analyzing your competition and knowing how you should position your business to differentiate it from the other caterers. First, identify any and all competitors, their strengths and weaknesses, and what kinds of events they serve and the foods they offer. Then, critically examine your proposed business and assess how it compares to the competition. Determine whether there are things you can change to give you a better advantage.

Finally, there are the practical matters. Part of your business plan involves a thorough understanding and identification of your sources of supplies, how you will promote your business, and how many people and what kind of positions will make up your staff. Catering is different from other small business operations because you are typically never working from a fixed site. This means you'll have to transport food, equipment, and people and plan accordingly.

Contracts

While somewhat imposing, to protect yourself and your clients, you will need to develop a catering contract. Contracts help clarify details so that all parties are clear about what is expected of them. Contracts should be written in clear, simple language that is void of legalese and that both parties understand. There is no specific format to contracts, but the following items are standard:

- Names and contact information for both the buyer and seller of services
- Dates of the agreement and date, time, and location of the event

- Event particulars, including setup, decorations, menu, and cleanup
- Number of guests being served and duration of the event
- Negotiated price, deposit, and payment schedule
- Cancellation policy
- Signatures of both parties (buyer and seller)

An online search using the keywords "catering" and "contract" will yield you numerous contracts to review and use as a boilerplate. Once you customize it according to the particulars of your business, be sure to have an attorney specializing in this area appraise it.

8

EDUCATION AND TRAINING

PREVIOUS CHAPTERS HAVE described the various positions available in the food service industry, some requiring little to no education, others requiring a bachelor's or master's degree. While the educational and training details specific to each type of job were given in those chapters, this chapter offers more general, but no less important, information necessary to prepare yourself for a career in food service. In addition to reading about the kinds of courses you should take at all levels of education, you'll read about ways in which you can fund your education through scholarships and grants, in addition to financial aid.

Education and training is necessary for advancement to positions of greater authority and compensation, and it is attainable by all. The more training and education you have, the better the opportunities available to you in the food service industry. Yet, no one in this field has to drop out of the running for lack of training or education.

High School

More than in many other industries, entry-level career opportunities exist in great variety in the food service industry. Indeed, any ambitious, hardworking, and career-minded individual can find a route to the top of the career ladder. A career in food service is well worth considering if you are a recent high school graduate who plans an immediate career start. It's also ideal for the individual who wishes to begin or change a career later in life or to finance an education.

Students can accelerate their food service career development by taking food service courses offered in high schools or vocational schools. Depending on the type and number of courses taken, these can give the graduate a slight advantage when seeking employment. Some pertinent courses include home economics, nutrition, and food planning and preparation. In addition, there are a variety of courses that, while not directly related to food service, will help you hone the skills necessary for a successful career. These include accounting, business management, communications, and computer science.

Part-time work in a food service job can be a valuable aid in getting your foot in the door. Many school districts, in cooperation with state departments of education, provide on-the-job training and summer workshops in cafeteria kitchens for those who aspire to become a cook. In addition, large corporations in the food service and hotel industries also offer paid internships and summer jobs, which can provide valuable experience and a nice paycheck!

No matter what level of education you've achieved, most food service operations are willing to invest time and money in training newcomers to the field. This is especially true of those who show enthusiasm for and dedication to the work. Once a person has gained a sound base of knowledge through on-the-job training, he or she can move upward into jobs with more responsibility and better pay.

ProStart Program

The ProStart program is an interesting opportunity offered by the National Restaurant Association Educational Foundation to high school students interested in a career in the food service industry. It is a nationwide network linking high schools and vocational schools with food service programs or courses to restaurants and other industry organizations so that students can get valuable on-the-job experience. There are currently approximately forty-four thousand students participating. The ProStart program has relationships with organizations in forty-four states, so there are sure to be opportunities near you. (See www.nraef.org/prostart for more details.)

Community College

A high school graduate can continue a food service program at a community college, four-year college, or culinary arts school. Upon completion of whichever program they choose, students will move on to a successful career. One of the richest sources of new management talent in the food service industry is found in community colleges that offer associate degrees in various aspects of food service. Hundreds of jobs are open to graduates with this training.

Two-year college programs pave the way for graduates to undertake a variety of beginning administrative and supervisory jobs in many types of food service operations. Some of the specific food service courses offered at community colleges include:

- Food purchasing and storage
- Food preparation
- Menu planning
- Equipment purchasing and layout
- Personnel management and job analysis
- Food standards and sanitation
- Diet therapy
- Catering
- Beverage control
- Food cost accounting
- Record keeping

In addition to the above, a number of general courses, designed to broaden the student's knowledge and outlook, will be required to earn an associate's degree. These classes include communications, psychology, sociology, economics, chemistry, and, of course, nutrition. It takes about two years of full-time study to earn an associate's degree from a community college.

There are several benefits to attending a community college. Most of these programs are less expensive than those at four-year colleges, and they often combine classroom work with practical job experience in part-time food service jobs. Many food service operators support their local college programs by providing part-time employment for students and also career opportunities for graduates. In addition, entrance requirements and fees tend to be minimal, which is good for those who had a less than outstanding high school career. Finally, community colleges are plentiful throughout every state, making them more accessible than four-year colleges. To locate one in your state, do an online search using the keywords "community college" or "food service" and your state.

Students not interested in an associate's degree can often enter a culinary arts certificate program offered by either the community college or a vocational or technical school. These programs are shorter in duration, and they teach students about a variety of topics, including food preparation, sanitation, nutrition, baking principles, and buffet and banquet techniques, among other things. Career paths and study of the hospitality industry are also frequently covered.

Four-Year University or College

Higher-level education is especially important for higher-level jobs, and holding a bachelor's or master's degree just might set you apart from the many others applying for your desired position. The food service industry's need for graduates with bachelor's degrees from four-year college programs in management has never really been filled. Increasingly, colleges and universities are also offering master's and doctoral degree programs in food service administration and restaurant and hotel management. There are numerous management and management-training positions that may require a degree from a four-year college, including:

- Assistant manager
- Food production supervisor
- Purchasing agent
- Food cost accountant
- Food service director
- Director of recipe development
- Sales manager
- Banquet manager

If you choose to attend a four-year school, you can expect intellectually challenging and stimulating classes in an atmosphere that places a greater emphasis on academics and intellectual discussions than on actual hands-on training—although that is also offered. For example, you may end up taking courses on culinary history and development or the cultural aspects of food, in addition to your more straightforward classes. Undergraduate programs include basic and advanced courses in food preparation; specialized courses in restaurant accounting, catering, management, and sanitation; and general courses in economics, law, marketing, cost control, and finance.

A requirement of many four-year colleges includes summer work in hotels, restaurants, and institutions. Many student associations at colleges and universities will also have a food service committee. Joining such a committee will not only look good on your future résumés, but it may offer you the opportunity to put into practice some of the skills you're learning in class.

Graduates of four-year programs receive bachelor's degrees in many different food service areas of specialty, including restaurant or institutional management, dietetics, home economics, business administration, the culinary arts, and travel and tourism.

There are literally thousands of choices of schools focusing on different aspects of the food service industry. When you are ready to select a school, you should speak to your high school or community college guidance counselor, write to the sources they suggest, and visit as many schools as you possibly can to develop an understanding of the choices available to you. After you have investigated all the possibilities, it is a good idea to discuss them with people in the field, who can offer you advice and help you evaluate your choices.

The Military

You've already read about the training and educational opportunities available to you through the military, but there are a few more things you should know to make an informed decision. To join the services, enlisted personnel must sign a legal agreement called an enlistment contract, which usually involves a commitment of up to eight years of service. Depending on the terms of the contract, two to six years are spent on active duty, and the balance is spent in the reserves. To enlist, one must be between seventeen and thirty-five years old, be a U.S. citizen or an alien holding permanent resident status, not have a felony record, and possess a birth certificate.

Applicants must pass both a written examination—the Armed Services Vocational Aptitude Battery—and meet certain minimum physical standards, such as height, weight, vision, and overall health. All branches of the armed forces require high school graduation or its equivalent for certain enlistment options. In 2003 nearly nine out of ten recruits were high school graduates.

The enlistment contract obligates the service to provide the agreed-upon job, rating, pay, cash bonuses for enlistment in certain occupations, medical and other benefits, occupational training, and continuing education. In return, enlisted personnel must serve satisfactorily for the period specified. Talk to a recruiter, who can determine whether you qualify for enlistment, explain the various enlistment options, and tell you which military occupational specialties currently have openings. Be sure to find out what the military can offer you, and what it will expect in return.

Ask the recruiter to assess your chances of being accepted for training in the occupation of your choice, or, better still, take the aptitude exam to see how well you score. The military uses this exam as a placement exam, and test scores largely determine an individual's chances of being accepted into a particular training program. Selection for a particular type of training depends on the needs of the service, your general and technical aptitudes, and your personal preference. Because all prospective recruits are required to take the exam, those who do so before committing themselves to enlist have the advantage of knowing in advance whether they stand a good chance of being accepted for training in a particular specialty.

The recruiter can schedule you for the Armed Services Vocational Aptitude Battery without any obligation. Many high schools offer the exam as an easy way for students to explore the possibility of a military career, and the test also affords an insight into career areas in which the student has demonstrated aptitudes and interests.

Following enlistment, new members of the armed forces undergo recruit training, better known as basic training. Through courses in military skills and protocol, recruit training provides a six- to twelve-week introduction to military life. Days and nights are carefully structured and include rigorous physical exercise designed to improve strength and endurance and build each unit's cohesion.

Following basic training, most recruits take additional training at technical schools that prepare them for a particular military occupational specialty. The formal training period generally lasts from ten to twenty weeks, although training for certain occupations—nuclear power plant operator, for example—may take as long as a year. Recruits not assigned to classroom instruction receive on-the-job training at their first duty assignment.

Many service people get college credit for the technical training they receive on duty, which, combined with off-duty courses, can lead to an associate's degree through programs in community colleges, such as the Community College of the Air Force. In addition to on-duty training, military personnel may choose from a variety of educational programs. Most military installations have tuition assistance programs for people who wish to take courses during off-duty hours. The courses may be correspondence courses or courses in degree programs offered by local colleges or universities. Tuition assistance pays up to 75 percent of college costs.

Also available are courses designed to help service personnel earn high school equivalency diplomas. Each branch of the service provides opportunities for full-time study to a limited number of exceptional applicants. Military personnel accepted into these highly competitive programs—in law or medicine, for example—receive full pay, allowances, tuition, and related fees. In return, they must agree to serve an additional amount of time in the service. Other highly selective programs enable enlisted personnel to qualify as commissioned officers through additional military training. Check out the Army Center of Excellence, Subsistence for more information on the kinds of training offered specifically to army recruits interested in food service at www.quartermaster.army .mil/aces/index.html.

Financing Your Education

If you are interested in pursuing education beyond high school, but are worried about financing it, have no fear; there are many different ways to finance your education. Scholarships and grants are possible for those in good academic standing, for those who belong to a particular religious or ethnic group, or for women. In addition, you can also finance your education through governmental student loans that you will be obligated to pay back upon graduation from your program.

In most cases, scholarship, financial aid, and grant funds are intended to supplement money earned during employment while also in school. For helpful information about all of these options, visit the Federal Student Aid website at http://studentaid.ed.gov. In addition to the scholarships listed below, you should conduct your own online search using pertinent keywords.

Many organizations and industry associations offer scholarships and grants. The National Restaurant Association Educational Foundation (NRAEF) makes many scholarships available to students of food service management, including hotel restaurant management, institutional management, dietetics, culinary arts, nutrition, food marketing, food science, and other food service curricula. To be eligible for scholarships, students are required to have full-time status for the full academic year beginning with the fall term, be enrolled full-time in a food service hospitality-related curriculum, and be pursuing an associate's, bachelor's, or master's degree.

Judging for these scholarships is based on a variety of factors, including industry work experience, academic standing, and views on the industry. In addition, the NRAEF offers educator work-study grants, which are awarded on a competitive basis to teachers and administrators of food service career education programs. The grants give recipients the chance to obtain work experience in the food service industry that will enrich and update their knowledge of the industry and thus increase their capability to impart that knowledge to students. Visit the NRAEF website (www.nraef.org) for more information on deadlines and application particulars. In addition, many state restaurant associations provide scholarships, and the National Restaurant Association provides links to state associations through its website at www.restaurant.org/states.

The American Culinary Federation is a nationwide association of professional chefs that offers continuing education, apprenticeship training, and scholarships. There are a number of educational scholarships available to those working in the hospitality industry, including the American Academy of Chefs Chair's Scholarship and the American Academy of Chefs Chaine des Rotisseurs Scholarship, as well as local chapter awards and corporate scholarships. Visit the ACF website at www.acfchefs.org/educate/eduschlr.html for more information.

The American Dietetic Association Foundation funds scholarships and awards, public awareness and research projects, and ADA strategic initiatives that promote optimal nutrition, health, and well-being of the public. It is the largest provider of scholarships and awards in the field of dietetics. Scholarship information can be found at www.eatright.org/public/7772.cfm.

The School Nutrition Association (SNA) plays an integral role in helping child nutrition professionals achieve their professional and educational goals by awarding several scholarships and grants. The GED Jump Start Scholarship provides eligible individuals with funds to pay for GED classes, GED study materials, and the GED test fee. The Nancy Curry scholarship is available to SNA members employed in school food service and their children who are pursuing undergraduate or graduate food service degrees at a vocational or technical school, community college, or four-year college or university. Schwan's Food Service scholarships are available to SNA members and their children who are pursuing formal education in a school food service–related field. Finally, the Child Nutrition Foundation Professional Growth scholarship is available to qualified SNA members who have successfully completed at least one course toward a master's degree. Additional information can be found at SNA's website at www.schoolnutrition.org; click first on the link for "Child Nutrition Foundation" and then "Academic Assistance."

The International Association of Culinary Professionals Foundation (IACPF) provides funds to qualified applicants for beginning, continuing, and specialty education courses at accredited culinary schools worldwide. In addition, individuals can receive scholarships for independent study for research projects. Check out the IACPF website at www.iacpfoundation.com/scholarships.html for additional information.

The International Foodservice Editorial Council (IFEC) offers scholarships for students preparing for food service communications careers. To be considered eligible for an award, you must be enrolled in a postsecondary, degree-granting educational institution and must show evidence of training, skill, and interest in both food service and the communication arts. Applicable majors in the communications area include journalism, public relations, mass communications, English, broadcast journalism, marketing, photography, graphic arts, and related studies. Visit the website at www.ifec-is-us.com/scholarship.htm for additional information.

Food and nutrition grants are available to qualified individuals from the U.S. government. Go to www.grants.gov and click on the link for "Find Grant Opportunities." From there you'll click on "Types of Grants" and then "Food and Nutrition." Subcategories in this section include food and nutrition for children, food inspection, food and nutrition for individuals and families, and research.

In general, to be considered by a scholarship committee, you must give specific and complete answers to all questions on the application form, and turn it in on or before the deadline. If a question does not apply, answer using the letters N/A (not applicable). You will need to have a letter of recommendation from your immediate supervisor, teacher, or college professor. In addition, you may have to provide transcripts and proof of registration.

Landing a Job in Food Service

Searching for jobs, applying to companies, and going on interviews can be a nerve-racking process—even for the most seasoned interviewee! However, there are steps you can take to ease your anxiety. Preparation is key to presenting a calm and confident appearance once you get the interview, but it's also necessary for submitting an eye-catching résumé that gets you called in to talk to someone in the first place. This chapter offers helpful tips and suggestions for embarking upon a successful job search. At the end of the chapter, you'll find a list of books for further information.

Knowing Yourself

Part of finding the best job for you, building your résumé, and having a successful interview is knowing yourself well. This means clearly identifying your current and future goals, ambitions, interests, talents, and skills. Sometimes, however, it is not easy to articulate all these things about yourself. The following exercise is designed to help you do just that. Using a piece of paper or on a computer, write down complete answers to the following twenty questions before you begin your job search.

1. What are your long-range career objectives? What do you see yourself doing five years from now?
2. What are the most important rewards you expect in your food service career?
3. Why did you choose the career for which you are preparing?
4. What is more important to you, the money or the type of job?
5. In your estimation, what are your greatest strengths and weaknesses?
6. How would you describe yourself? How would a friend describe you? A professor?
7. What motivates you to put forth your greatest effort?
8. How has your past experience prepared you for your career?
9. Why should someone hire you?
10. What personal qualifications make you think you will be successful in your career?
11. How do you evaluate or determine success?
12. How can you contribute to a particular company?
13. What should be the relationship between a supervisor and those reporting to him or her?
14. Name two or three accomplishments that have given you the most satisfaction. Why?
15. What school subject did you like best and least? Why?
16. Do you have plans for continued study?
17. What is your most comfortable work environment?

18. Why did you choose to seek a position with this particular company?
19. What do you know about this company?
20. Do you have a geographical preference? Why?

Steps to Success

For the past several years and projected well into the future, there is expected to be an abundance of available positions in the food industry. Some jobs, however, are more limited than others, and all jobs must be approached with the same level of professionalism. As mentioned above, the key to success is planning and preparation—from beginning the job search to following up after the interview. Here's a list of twelve steps that will help you through the process:

1. Determine what kind of position you desire and are best suited for.
2. Plan a step-by-step campaign for securing that job.
3. Prepare a polished résumé and cover letter.
4. Network by informing coworkers, high school or college placement officers, purveyors, private employment agencies, and friends that you are seeking employment in this field. Ask if they have any good leads.
5. Secure all the information you can about companies that you are interested in by talking with people and conducting online research.
6. Write a letter to each company and enclose a résumé for consideration if you know there's a job opening; or, place telephone calls to administrative assistants or human resources departments inquiring about employment opportunities.

7. Arrange for an interview.

8. Prepare for the interview, both in mental attitude and by physical appearance.

9. Go to the interview prepared with a list of questions about the company (after all, you're interviewing them, too!) and with targeted selling points about you.

10. Appraise yourself after the interview. Evaluate your answers to the interviewer's questions, analyze your performance, and correct any negative statements so you can do better in future interviews.

11. Write a thank-you letter to the interviewer for the time and consideration given you.

12. Wait to hear from the company on the specified date; if you don't hear by then, contact the company.

The following sections in this chapter offer greater details about each phase of the job search process, starting with researching potential positions.

Finding the Perfect Job

Word-of-mouth or networking is a great way to hear about food service positions. In fact, you are more likely to be hired by a company if someone who currently works there recommends you. This does not mean that you have to be best buddies with the person who passes along your résumé; you don't even have to know him or her other than through an introduction by a mutual acquaintance. Sending a general e-mail out to all your friends and relatives, letting them know you're looking for a job and which sector of the industry is of the greatest interest to you is a start.

Of course, you don't want to send a general e-mail to persons in the industry. To make industry-specific contacts, you should use the Internet to locate companies that are appealing to you and find out the name of the person in charge of the specific department in which you want to work. Call or e-mail the person, state who you are and your interest in the company, and ask if you can come in for a brief, informational interview. If he or she agrees, make sure you dress as if it were a real interview, come prepared with a list of intelligent questions, take up no more than a half hour of the person's time, try to get contact information for other people to speak with either with that company or another, and leave a copy of your résumé with the informational interviewer when you leave.

As you might have guessed, networking involves forming a network of friends, former teachers, business acquaintances, and anyone else who could help provide you with information leading to a job in the food service industry. Stay organized by making a list of all the people you know who might be able to help you, along with their contact information. You should have a note section that allows you to keep track of when and how you contacted them, the substance of the correspondence, and what follow-up, if any, is required. Keep in touch with industry-types regularly, and ask if they have come across any leads; e-mail is particularly good for this kind of contact as it is fairly low-pressure; just make sure that your e-mails are also polished and professional.

Outside the industry, those who know the owners and managers of places where you want to work are also valuable. Don't hesitate to ask them to keep you informed of job openings, and ask them, in advance, if it is OK to use their names as a means of securing an introduction or interview. No matter who you are speaking with, always be sure to thank your contacts, whether they are able to steer you to a job or not; their interest in and knowledge of you as a learner and a worker can be very valuable to you in other, future job searches as well.

There are a variety of ways to locate job openings in addition to networking. Professional associations (see Appendix A) usually have listings posted on their websites. Newspapers, professional journals, and trade magazines typically have sections that feature classified ads of a variety of positions. The Internet is perhaps the best source of information for researching openings at companies you've identified as good prospects and for browsing job-search websites. Popular job search websites include America's Job Bank (www.job search.org), Career Builder (www.careerbuilder.com), College Grad (www.collegegrad.com), Food Service (www.foodservice.com), Hot Jobs (www.hotjobs.com), JobWeb.com (www.jobweb.com), and Monster (www.monster.com). The Yellow Pages phone directory is a good place to identify different types of businesses in the food service industry, but you won't find a listing of available jobs. You'll need to do further research either online or by calling the human resources department or general phone line to inquire about the availability of positions. Contact pertinent unions or view their websites (see Appendix A) to find specific positions when you've identified your area of interest. Finally, you may want to consider private employment agencies and recruiters, who take on the work of searching for positions and lining up interviews.

While you are looking for your ideal position and networking, you should also begin the process of putting together a superior résumé and cover letter, or update and polish your current one. Interviews may come faster than you think, so it's good to get started on building your résumé and cover letter as early as possible. The following section offers advice to help you do just that.

Building a Résumé and Cover Letter

Some people find putting together a résumé and cover letter to be quite painful, but there are tools to help make the job a bit easier. Many word processing programs, such as Microsoft Word, have résumé templates that act as a guide for the kind of information you need to include. In addition, these programs plug your information into an attractive design. There are plenty of sources, both in print and online, for additional information on the construction of your résumé and cover letter. Many of these sources—some of which are featured at the end of this chapter—also offer sample résumés pertinent to the field. The main thing to keep in mind for those building résumés and cover letters for the food industry is not to get too fancy or too creative. These documents are for informational purposes, and while they should also be pleasing to the eye, the cover letter should not be humorous or cute and the résumé should not turn into a graphic designer's portfolio!

The purpose of a résumé is to organize the relevant facts about you and your educational and job history in a clear and concise written presentation. Your résumé should contain brief but sufficient information to inform a prospective employer about the following:

- Your abilities and talents
- Your accomplishments
- Your knowledge
- The desired position

By providing this information, your résumé will accomplish several important objectives. It will present an overview of your skills and experience. It will save time for you—the applicant—and the interviewer; you will not have to spend a lot of time discussing where you worked and when, because it is all on the résumé. The interviewer can use the résumé as a guide to the interview, so be sure to include all of your accomplishments, presenting them in such a way that compels the interviewer to ask about them. Further, when your assets are organized on paper, it will be easier to discuss them with assurance, and fumbling for dates and significant facts will be eliminated. Finally, the résumé provides the interviewer with a visual reminder of what you covered verbally during the interview.

When you start to construct your résumé, first write down the basics and then move on to jazzing up the wording with more compelling language. The heading should consist of your name and contact information in bold print. The position for which you are applying can either be specified in the résumé in the "Objective" section or in the body of the cover letter that accompanies the résumé. Next follows either your education or experience, depending on which is more of a selling tool for you. Then list any scholarships, grants, or awards you've received, such as employee of the month; pertinent associations or organizations you belong to; or volunteer activities. Finally, the phrase "References Available on Request" should also be included at the end of the résumé. You do not need to list your references here, but you should have them available to hand out on an interview on a separate sheet of paper. One word of warning: be sure to contact each person and get permission to use her or him as a reference.

The résumé is not merely a functional piece of paper that lists your contact information, education, and the jobs you've held; the résumé is also a selling tool that markets your skills and talents and positions you for a job in your area of interest. That is why the use of the active voice and a variety of compelling words is so important. Think of it this way: would you rather buy the bran cereal that positions itself as "full of fiber that adds bulk to your diet" or "rich in heart-healthy fiber that will fill you up and help you lose weight—delicious AND nutritious!" Create a list of compelling and selling words and phrases that will help you construct your résumé. For example, are you energetic, hardworking, enthusiastic, or quick to learn? Have you ever been responsible for or in charge of anything? Have you worked in fast-paced or dynamic environments?

In some cases, the cover letter will be read even before your résumé, so it is vital that you use correct grammar and punctuation, the title for the person to whom you're writing, and strong language that sells yourself to your potential employer. Again, there are many guides for writing a good cover letter; in general, however, you should include the following:

- The purpose of your inquiry, including the title of the position you're applying for, stated up front
- The name of the person who referred you to the position, if applicable
- Your pertinent job-related or educational experience
- Why you would be a good addition to the company
- If you will follow up (and when) or wait to hear back from someone
- An expression of appreciation for the person's time and effort in considering you as a candidate

The final step in polishing your résumé and cover letter is making sure that they are error-free. Be sure to use the spell-check feature in your word processing program. Go over your documents very carefully to be sure that they read smoothly and make sense, and have a friend who is good with grammar look them over for you. Above all, make sure the name and title of the person to whom you're directing your cover letter are correct.

Interviewing Basics

You feel a rush of excitement when you get the call that a prospective employer would like you to come in for an interview, followed by gnawing anxiety. This is only natural—everyone feels this way. The first thing to do is take a deep breath, exhale, and congratulate yourself for getting to this point. The only thing between now and your first paycheck is a simple conversation, albeit a very important one. Keeping things in perspective will help you keep your cool when it comes to the interview.

At heart, the interview is a conversation in which the interviewer or employer is trying to get a sense of whether the interviewee or employee is a good fit for both the company and the position, and vice versa. If you believe, based on what you've found out about the company, that you are the best candidate for the position, then it is now your job to convince the interviewer of this. Prior to the interview, you should do as much research as possible about the company so that you will appear eager and well informed during the interview. Do an online search of the company and peruse its website, if there is one. Note any interesting, recent news about the company or products it produces that you can bring up and talk about during the interview.

While you're doing this, try to think of intelligent questions you can ask since there is almost always a point during the conversation when the interviewer will ask if you have any. You might want to ask about opportunities for promotion within the company or if the company has any plans for expansion. This shows that you are forward thinking and interested in having a future with the company.

During the interview, while you may be nervous, try not to show it. It's best to project a calm, confident manner. Smile and make plenty of eye contact. Bring your résumé and references with you in a nice binder or briefcase, if you have one. Thank the interviewer up front for giving you the opportunity to come in and talk to him or her. Be prepared to discuss why you think you're the best person for this position, and don't be shy about expressing your interest; enthusiasm is contagious and your interviewer will respond to it. At the end of your interview, thank the person again and make sure you get a specific date by which you will hear from him or her. Follow up the interview with a thank-you note mentioning something specific that came up during the interview to help the interviewer remember you. The following are several tips to keep in mind to help you have a successful interview:

- Be on time for your interview. Punctuality is a must in this industry.
- First impressions are very important. Treat all those you meet, as well as your interviewer, politely and respectfully.
- Dress appropriately for the interview. Even if you won't dress up on the job, it is essential that you do so for an interview.
- A complete application is an important part of the interview process. Be sure to answer every question thoroughly and neatly.
- If you possess any special skills or talents, include them on the application. There may be a special position just for you.

- Show interest in the company, sit up straight, and maintain eye contact. One-word responses to questions, gum chewing, and smoking before the interview should be avoided.
- Don't be reluctant to ask questions. It's a sign of interest and enthusiasm.

Additional Resources

Bermont, Todd. *Insider Secrets to a Winning Job Search: Everything You Need to Get the Job You Want in 24 Hours—Or Less.* Franklin Lakes, N.J.: Career Press, 2004.

Jansen, Julie. *I Don't Know What I Want, but I Know It's Not This: A Step-by-Step Guide to Finding Gratifying Work.* New York: Penguin, 2003.

Messmer, Max. *Job-Hunting for Dummies.* Foster City, Calif.: John Wiley & Sons, Inc., 1999. (There are numerous relevant titles in this series, including *Job Interviews for Dummies*, *Résumés for Dummies*, and *Cover Letters for Dummies*, all by Joyce Lain Kennedy, and *Job Searching Online for Dummies* by Pam Dixon.)

Nelson Bolles, Richard, and Mark Emery Bolles. *What Color is Your Parachute? 2005: A Practical Manual for Job-Hunters and Career-Changers.* Berkeley, Calif.: Ten Speed Press, 2004.

Riley Dikel, Margaret, and Frances E. Roehm. *Guide to Internet Job Searching 2004–2005.* New York: McGraw-Hill, 2004.

Stafford, Diane, and Moritza Day. *1000 Best Job-Hunting Secrets.* Naperville, Ill.: Sourcebooks, 2004.

Taylor, Jeffrey, and Douglas Hardy. *Monster Careers: How to Land the Job of Your Life.* New York: Penguin, 2004.

Yate, Martin. *Knock 'em Dead 2005: The Ultimate Job Seeker's Guide.* Holbrook, Mass.: Adams Media, 2004.

Appendix A

Professional Associations

The following is a list of international, national, and state associations to contact for further information on opportunities in food service careers.

National and International

American Association of Franchisees and Dealers
P.O. Box 81887
San Diego, CA 92138
www.aafd.org

American Beverage Institute
1775 Pennsylvania Ave. NW, Ste. 1200
Washington, DC 20006
www.abionline.org

American Culinary Federation
180 Center Place Way
St. Augustine, FL 32095
www.acfchefs.org

American Dietetic Association
120 S. Riverside Plaza, Ste. 2000
Chicago, IL 60606
www.eatright.org

American Franchisee Association
53 W. Jackson Blvd., Ste. 1157
Chicago, IL 60604
www.franchisee.org

American Hotel and Lodging Association
1201 New York Ave. NW, Ste. 600
Washington, DC 20005
www.ahla.com

American Institute of Wine and Food
1303 Jefferson St., Ste. 100-B
Napa, CA 94559
www.aiwf.org

American Management Association
1601 Broadway
New York, NY 10019
www.amanet.org

American Society for Healthcare Food Service Administrators
304 W. Liberty St., Ste. 201
Louisville, KY 40202
www.ashfsa.org

Best Management Practices Center of Excellence
4321 Hartwick Rd., Ste. 400
College Park, MD 20740
www.bmpcoe.org

Commercial Food Equipment Service Association
2211 W. Meadowview Rd., Ste. 20
Greensboro, NC 27407
www.cfesa.com

Commission on Dietetic Registration
120 S. Riverside Plaza, Ste. 2000
Chicago, IL 60606
www.cdrnet.org

Council of Hotel and Restaurant Trainers
P.O. Box 2835
Westfield, NJ 07091
www.chart.org

Food Marketing Institute
655-15th St. NW
Washington, DC 20005
www.fmi.org

Food Service and Packaging Institute
150 S. Washington St., Ste. 204
Falls Church, VA 22046
www.fpi.org

Foodservice Consultants Society International
304 W. Liberty St., Ste. 201
Louisville, KY 40202-3068
www.fcsi.org

Hotel Employees and Restaurant Employees International Union
275 Seventh Ave.
New York, NY 10001
www.unitehere.org

International Association of Culinary Professionals
304 W. Liberty St., Ste. 201
Louisville, KY 40202
www.iacp.com

International Council on Hotel, Restaurant, and Institutional
   Education
2613 N. Parham Rd., 2nd Fl.
Richmond, VA 23294
www.chrie.org

International Dairy-Deli-Bakery Association
P.O. Box 5528
Madison, WI 53705-0528
www.iddba.org

International Food Services Executives Association
836 San Bruno Ave.
Henderson, NV 89015
www.ifsea.org

International Foodservice Manufacturers Association
101-23 Lesmill Rd.
Don Mills, ON
Canada M3B 3P6
www.foodserviceworld.com

International Franchise Association
1350 New York Ave. NW, Ste. 900
Washington, DC 20005
www.franchise.org

National Association of College and University Food Services
1405 S. Harrison, Ste. 305
Manly Miles Building, MSU
East Lansing, MI 48824
www.nacufs.org

National Frozen and Refrigerated Foods Association
4755 Linglestown Rd., Ste. 300
P.O. Box 6069
Harrisburg, PA 17112
www.nfraweb.org

National Military Family Association
2500 N. Van Dorn St., Ste. 102
Alexandria, VA 22302
www.nmfa.org

National Park Hospitality Association
3701 Court House Dr.
Ellicott City, MD 21043
www.nphassn.org

National Restaurant Association
1200 Seventeenth St. NW
Washington, DC 20036
www.restaurant.org
(access state restaurant associations through this site)

National Restaurant Association Educational Foundation
175 W. Jackson Blvd., Ste. 1500
Chicago, IL 60604
www.nraef.org

National Small Business Association
1156-15th St. NW, Ste. 1100
Washington, DC 20005
www.nsba.biz

North American Association of Food Equipment Manufacturers
161 N. Clark St., Ste. 2020
Chicago, IL 60601
www.nafem.org

Produce Marketing Association
1500 Casho Mill Rd.
P.O. Box 6036
Newark, DE 19714
www.pma.com

School Nutrition Association
700 S. Washington St., Ste. 300
Alexandria, VA 22314
www.schoolnutrition.org

Service Employees International Union
1313 L St. NW
Washington, DC 20005
www.seiu.org

Small Business Development Center
8990 Burke Lake Rd.
Burke, VA 22015
www.asbdc-us.org

Society for Foodservice Management
304 W. Liberty St., Ste. 201
Louisville, KY 40202
www.sfm-online.org

Travel Industry Association of America
1100 New York Ave., Ste. 450
Washington, DC 20005
www.tia.org

United Food and Commercial Workers International Union
1775 K St. NW
Washington, DC 20006
www.ufcw.org

United States Small Business Administration
409 Third St. SW
Washington, DC 20416
www.sba.gov

United States Sommelier Association
P.O. Box 402312
Miami Beach, FL 33140
www.ussommelier.com

Wine Institute
425 Market St., Ste. 1000
San Francisco, CA 94105
www.wineinstitute.org

Women Chefs and Restaurateurs
304 W. Liberty St., Ste. 201
Louisville, KY 40202
www.womenchefs.org

State

For states that are not mentioned below, look on the National
Restaurant Association's website at www.restaurant.org.

Arkansas Hospitality Association
P.O. Box 3866
603 S. Pulaski St.
Little Rock, AR 72203
www.arhospitality.org

Restaurant and Hospitality Association of Indiana
200 S. Meridian St., Ste. 350
Indianapolis, IN 46225
www.indianarestaurants.org

Iowa Hospitality Association
8525 Douglas Ave., Ste. 47
Des Moines, IA 50322
www.iowahospitality.com

Kansas Restaurant and Hospitality Association
3500 N. Rock Rd., Bldg. 1300
Wichita, KS 67226
www.krha.org

Hospitality Minnesota
305 E. Roselawn Ave.
St. Paul, MN 55117
www.hospitalitymn.com

Mississippi Hospitality and Restaurant Association
P.O. Box 16395
Jackson, MS 39236
www.msra.org

New Hampshire Lodging and Restaurant Association
P.O. Box 1175
14 Dixon Ave., Ste. 208
Concord, NH 03302
www.nhlra.com

North Dakota Hospitality Association
1025 N. Third St.
Bismarck, ND 58501
www.ndhospitality.com

Rhode Island Hospitality and Tourism Association
832 Dyer Ave.
Cranston, RI 02920
www.rihospitality.org

Hospitality Association of South Carolina
3612 Landmark Dr.
Columbia, SC 29204
www.schospitality.org

Vermont Lodging and Restaurant Association
13 Kilburn St.
Burlington, VT 05401
www.visitvt.com

Virginia Hospitality and Travel Association
2101 Libbie Ave.
Richmond, VA 23230
www.vhta.org

West Virginia Hospitality and Travel Association
P.O. Box 2391
Charleston, WV 25328
www.wvhta.com

Wyoming Lodging and Restaurant Association
211 W. Nineteenth St.
P.O. Box 1003
Cheyenne, WY 82001
www.wlra.org

Appendix B

Industry Trade Periodicals

Baking Mangement
Penton Media, Inc.
1300 E. 9th St.
Cleveland, OH 44114
http://bakingmanagement.bakery-net.com

Beverage World
VNU Business Publications
770 Broadway
New York, NY 10003
www.beverageworld.com

Chain Leader
360 Park Ave. South
New York, NY 10014
www.foodservice411.com

Cooking for Profit
P.O. Box 267
Fond du Lac, WI 54936
www.cookingforprofit.com

Cornell Hotel and Restaurant Administration Quarterly
Sage Publications
2455 Teller Rd.
Thousand Oaks, CA 91320
www.hotelschool.cornell.edu/publications

Food Management
Penton Publications
1300 E. 9th St.
Cleveland, OH 44114
www.food-management.com

Food Manufacturing
Reed Business Information
100 Enterprise Dr., Ste. 600
Rockaway, NJ 07886
www.foodmanufacturing.com

Food Review
Economic Research Service, U.S. Department of Agriculture
1800 M St. NW
Washington, DC 20036
www.ers.usda.gov/publications/foodreview/archives

Foodservice Director
Bill Communications
355 Park Ave. South
New York, NY 10010
www.fsdmag.com

Foodservice Equipment and Supplies
360 Park Ave. South
New York, NY 10014
www.foodservice411.com

Gourmet Retailer (e-newsletter)
www.gourmetretailer.com

Journal of Child Nutrition and Management
700 S. Washington St., Ste. 300
Alexandria, VA 22314
www.schoolnutrition.org

Journal of Management
Terry College of Business
University of Georgia
Athens, GA 30602
www.journalofmanagement.org

Modern Baking
Penton Media, Inc.
1300 E. 9th St.
Cleveland, OH 44114
http://modernbaking.bakery-net.com

Nation's Restaurant News
3922 Coconut Palm Dr.
Tampa, FL 33619
www.nrn.com

Pizza Today
908 S. 8th St., Ste. 200
Louisville, KY 40203
www.pizzatoday.com

Prepared Foods Magazine
1050 IL Route 83, Ste. 200
Bensenville, IL 60106
www.preparedfoods.com

Restaurant Economic Trends
National Restaurant Association
1200 17th St. NW
Washington, DC 20036
www.restaurant.org

Restaurant Hospitality
Penton Media, Inc.
1300 E. 9th St.
Cleveland, OH 44114
www.restaurant-hospitality.com

Restaurant and Institutions
360 Park Ave. South
New York, NY 10014
www.foodservice411.com

School Foodservice and Nutrition
700 S. Washington St., Ste. 300
Alexandria, VA 22314
www.schoolnutrition.org

About the Author

Carol Caprione Chmelynski began her food service career in 1976 with the National Milk Producers Federation. She went on to become an editorial assistant at the Food Marketing Institute and later worked as a communications specialist at the National Restaurant Association in Washington, DC, where she wrote feature articles for the association's monthly magazine, *NRA News*. That magazine was subsequently titled *Restaurants USA*. While the magazine is out of print as of 2002, back issues are still available online at www.restaurant.org/rusa.

Ms. Chmelynski worked as a copywriter for the advertising firm of Stackig, Sanderson, and White in McLean, Virginia, where she wrote product as well as job recruitment ads for high-technology companies such as Electronic Data Systems, Network Solutions, Tempest Technologies, and Capital Systems Group, Inc.

Currently, Ms. Chmelynski is the assistant managing editor of *School Board News*, a biweekly newspaper of the National School Boards Association in Alexandria, Virginia.